GENDER DIFFERENCES
AT WORK

GENDER DIFFERENCES AT WORK

WOMEN AND MEN IN NONTRADITIONAL OCCUPATIONS

CHRISTINE L. WILLIAMS

University of California Press

Berkeley · Los Angeles · London

University of California Press
Berkeley and Los Angeles, California

University of California Press, Ltd.
London, England

© 1989 by
The Regents of the University of California

Library of Congress Cataloging-in-Publication Data

Williams, Christine L.
  Gender differences at work: women and men in
nontraditional occupations / Christine L. Williams.
    p.   cm.
  Bibliography: p.
  Includes index.
  ISBN 0-520-06373-2 (alk. paper)
  1. Sex role in the work environment—United States.
2. United States. Marine Corps—Women.   3. Women and the
military—United States.   4. Men nurses—United States.
5. Stereotype (Psychology)
I. Title.
HD6060.5.U5W55 1989
305.3—dc19
                                                88-10778
                                                CIP

Printed in the United States of America

1   2   3   4   5   6   7   8   9

For Martin

Contents

Foreword

Neil J. Smelser

Those who read the pages that follow will discover an ingenious work. It is a special variant of what Mary Douglas (1986) refers to as "back-door" research, or the study of social order when it breaks down or otherwise experiences deviations from its main organizing principles. She mentions in particular the experiments of Harold Garfinkel (1967), who instructed his students to act as stooges and cheat in games, to haggle over prices in a supposedly "one-price" market, and at home to behave toward their parents as though they were their house guests rather than their children. These disruptive encounters, of course, underscored the power of established rules and understandings, as well as the immediate, powerful impulse of the affected actors to restore things to their supposedly proper order.

In a special sense Dr. Williams's research constitutes an example of this genre. She has taken two occupations typed by gender, populated accordingly, and gender-centric in the extreme: the United States Marine Corps and the profession of nursing. The marines have carried an image of "masculine" toughness and discipline, a preoccupation with masculine symbols, such as guns and muscles, a sense of masculine pride and honor, and a kind of phobia about non-warlike and "feminine" sentiments, such as gentleness and love. Nursing, with some historical exceptions (such as the American Civil War, when male nurses were common), has been a basically feminine profession, emphasizing care and comfort and deriving its name from the ultimately feminine act of offering the breast to the suckling infant. In modern times, however, these extremes have broken down a little as a few women have entered the Marine Corps and a few men have taken up nursing. Dr. Williams has taken advantage of these exceptional developments to study a sample of these two minorities. In this sense, her study is "back-door" research: it picks up the experiences of the few who have begun to break down the largely "gender-pure" institutions.

How have these special minorities fared in their respective special positions? It is difficult to provide a general answer to this question because the sample studied by Dr. Williams is admittedly neither large nor representative; even in such a sample a good deal of variation among female marines and male nurses can be observed. One impression that remains, however, is this: At the level of conscious comfort or discomfort in their lives, female marines seem to fare better than male nurses, despite the fact that the former are subjected to all kinds of discrimination and abuse to their feminine identity, whereas men are not and apparently enjoy a certain number of objective advantages over female nurses. A superficial but telling index of this fact (if it is a fact) is the different responses to Dr. Williams's efforts to contact subjects and interview them. She was openly received and given every kind of cooperation in her contacts with female marines (I even heard of a few scattered efforts to recruit *her* into the marines), whereas there was a measure of resistance and defensiveness on the part of male nurses; the one exception to this was her welcome into a male nurses' organization, a gesture, however, that had an instrumental note in that her presence was used as part of an ongoing campaign for status-enrichment. The reasons for this difference are no doubt many, not the least of which might be the fact that the investigator was a woman. Be that as it may, Dr. Williams's major explanation, consistent with psychoanalytic theories of differential development and identity formation, is that "adult men are more concerned than women with establishing and defending their gender identity," and, by implication, would be more threatened in a role that is so clearly identified with the other gender. I will return briefly to the question of psychodynamics in these kinds of situations, after a few words on the use of the psychoanalytic perspective.

This is not the first time that the microscopic psychoanalytic perspective has been brought to bear on the explanation of macroscopic phenomena. The field of "culture and personality" was in large part the application of psychoanalytic insights to the study of cultural and institutional forms. The psychoanalytic perspective has also been brought successfully to bear on the analysis of cultural productions, particularly literary forms. And the field of psychohistory is in large part an effort to show the impact of psychoanalytically informed biographies on the course of historical events. As far as I know, however, Dr. Williams's book is a pioneering effort to bring that perspective directly to bear on the analysis of roles in society.

First, it is difficult to apply the psychoanalytic perspective in a research project such as this. As Dr. Williams herself acknowledges, the kind of interviews carried out really do not lend themselves to psychoanalytic interpretations—unconscious identifications, resentments, and loves of parents and siblings in the developmental years, as well as defenses against anxieties and conflict that may be associated with these. Considerations of privacy and confidentiality generally discourage the eliciting of such information in research interviews, and even if asked directly, respondents are unlikely to have access to or insights about psychological processes, which are largely unconscious and reveal themselves only in clinical situations with free association, analysis of transference feelings, and the like. For this reason, Dr. Williams can, and does, make the case that much of the data she has uncovered is consistent with the psychoanalytic perspective she has chosen and not so consistent with other explanations; but she cannot move much further toward strong confirmation.

As indicated, the main range of psychoanalytic insights Dr. Williams employs is the socialization perspective put forward initially by Parsons (1955) and later extended and elaborated by Chodorow (1978), to the effect that men in our society are required to move further away than women from the state of infantile maternal dependency. Men may pay a greater psychological price on that account and generally have a more fragile gender identification that is more in need of shoring up, asserting, and defending. This perspective certainly accounts for the seeming paradox that female marines, who objectively suffer from greater gender disadvantage than male nurses, are more comfortable with their femininity than the latter are with their masculinity. I would imagine, however, that their respective psychological stories are more complex than this, and I would like to speculate for a moment on that score.

When asked why they joined the marines, women responded by and large with pragmatic answers having to do with financial and emotional security; male nurses also stressed the pragmatics of financial security, that their choice was a second-best to being a medical doctor, and so on. These responses, which must be taken at their word, certainly have little to do with the standard psychoanalytic explanation that people are drawn—or draw themselves—into major life situations such as marriage or career as arenas in which they continue to work out their neurotic conflicts and their defenses against them. We do not know from Dr. Williams's interview material whether or not these latter agendas were active, although perhaps unconscious, elements in her respondents' career decisions. Whether or not this is the case, it remains clear that, once in their respective settings, female marines and male nurses find themselves in situations in which very fundamental conflicts are certainly and continuously activated.

Female marines, for example, are constantly exposed to the

message that they are not men—and are the less for that—by degradation rituals, ridicule, and denial of access to male preroga-tives having to do with guns and violence. They are sometimes exposed to the message that they may not be very good women either; male stereotypes about lesbianism and promiscuity persist. Male nurses do not suffer the discriminatory abuses and indigni-ties, but they are daily thrust into situations in which they are expected to be caring if not loving; and they, too, live under the persistent stigma of possibly or probably being homosexual. For both groups, there is that vague and constantly irritating expecta-tion that eyebrows will be raised, or surprise or threat registered, when others learn of their occupation. There is also some vague pressure on both male nurses and female marines to account some-how for their anomalous choice of career.

What kinds of conflicts are likely to emerge from these situa-tions? Sigmund Freud's observation in one of his latest works, "Analysis Terminable and Interminable" (1964 [1937]), comes to mind. Toward the end of this essay, he commented, in a pessimis-tic mode:

> At no other point in one's analytic work does one suffer more from an oppressive feeling that all one's repeated efforts have been in vain, and from a suspicion that one has been "preaching to the winds," than when one is trying to persuade a woman to abandon her wish for a penis on the ground of its being unrealizable or when one is seeking to convince a man that a passive attitude to men does not always signify castration and that it is indispensable in many relations in life. The rebellious overcompensation of the male produces one of the strongest transference-resistances. . . . No analogous transference can arise from the female's wish for a penis, but it is the source of outbreaks of severe depression in her, owing to an internal conviction that the analysis will be of no use and that nothing can be done to help her. (252)

To call to mind this reason for the "interminability" of analysis is not to revive the notion that penis envy and castration anxiety are the two great psychological moving principles for women and men, respectively, as Freud thought them to be; that extreme position has been appropriately discredited both within and outside of psychoanalytic circles. In the situations of both female marines and male nurses, however, such conflicts are activated by the circumstances of their careers, in which women are continually reminded that they are not men in dozens of ways—including the most obviously symbolic one that they cannot shoot guns to kill people—and men are being reminded that they are doing women's work. That is to say, the conflicts in question are situationally evoked, independent of their psychological status, as a result of the socialization experiences of the relevant actors.

In any event, we must acknowledge with Dr. Williams that for reasons found both in socialization and situational experiences of female marines and male nurses, those roles will not be without severe conflicts about gender and identification. What, we might ask, finally, are the kinds of defenses that are arrayed to contend with such conflicts? Such a question is difficult to answer, too, because of the methodological reasons cited before. Nevertheless, one might speculate that there are some differences between women in male-dominated roles and men in female-dominated roles, but also one similarity. These speculations are based on Dr. Williams's own data.

For female marines, one observable type of adaptation is identification with the aggressor. There are certainly a lot of aggressors in the marines, and many of them occupy superior positions to those of female marines. When interviewed about their segregation and their subordinated status, some female marines objected to it, but others found a certain logic to it and favored the inequality. The other major defense that struck me as plausible is the female marines' splitting the conflict (along with practicing a certain denial) that enables them to be perfectly comfortable as both a marine and a woman. Dr. Williams argues that this is more nearly possible for women because of their particular socialization; but I would suspect there is a defensiveness at work here as well. The picture for male nurses is less clear, but I suspect that the denial of femininity (a powerful mechanism) is central—

homosexual male nurses would constitute a complicated case exception. Another mechanism might be termed a kind of resentful projection, by which male nurses attribute uncomfortable things about their positions to the fact that they are working in a woman's profession, and that circumstances prevent them from reaching the career and status levels to which they aspire.

For both female marines and male nurses it is possible to see one common thread: a reassertion of gender identification. I mentioned the premium on remaining a woman while also a marine; in addition, female marines apparently readily accept— and desire—differentiating gender-related practices such as the use of cosmetics. Finally, most seem to have fairly traditional marital and mothering expectations. As a rule, male nurses tend to skew their role performances in a variety of ways in order to move them in a more "masculine" direction (e.g., dealing with violent situations and doing heavier lifting work). In addition, there is some evidence that some identify more with male doctors. In these cases as well, the behavior would appear to have elements of both the expected reemergence of gender characteristics acquired in the socialization process and a defensive reaction to the uncomfortable aspects of their unusual situations.

These few observations having been put forward, it remains only to welcome Christine Williams's exciting and important work, to confirm that it is most seminal and will no doubt stimulate much work of its kind, and to welcome her as an already accomplished and very promising young sociologist.

Acknowledgments

This book began as my dissertation at the University of California, Berkeley. Neil Smelser, my thesis advisor, directed the original study and provided intellectual guidance and moral support through every stage of its development. I am also indebted to Nancy Chodorow, whose ground-breaking work on psychoanalysis and gender sparked the original idea for this study. Her expertise in feminist theory and qualitative methodology was extremely helpful in designing this study and framing its central questions.

Many friends helped me at various stages of this project. This work has benefited enormously from my innumerable discussions with Kenneth Bock, Mary Waters, and Judy Auerbach. I also gratefully acknowledge the advice I received from Jimmy Christiana, Robert A. Nye, Nancy Scheper-Hughes, and Terry Strathman.

I credit Naomi Schneider, my editor at the University of California Press, with transforming my dissertation into this book. Her unswerving confidence in this project sustained me through countless revisions.

Finally, I owe a sincere debt of gratitude to all the people who shared their thoughts and work experiences with me. In particular, I wish to thank the leadership of the Women Marines' Association, the Public Relations Office and the Women Recruit Training Command at the Parris Island Marine Corps Training Depot, and the American Assembly for Men in Nursing, particularly Dr. Luther Christman. In addition, I owe special thanks to the Department of Sociology and the Graduate Division, University of California, Berkeley, for funding portions of this research.

I

Introduction

Picture in your mind a female drill sergeant in the United States
Marine Corps. Do you imagine a muscular, gruff, masculine
woman? Now picture a male nurse. Does a gentle, effeminate
image come to mind?

The military and the nursing profession are intimately linked to
stereotypes about gender. We assume that the Marine Corps demands of its soldiers certain "masculine" traits—strength, aggressiveness, emotional detachment; we assume that nursing requires
"feminine" qualities—nurturing, caring, and passivity. Many believe that only men are naturally suited for the Marine Corps and
only women for nursing. Exceptions—women in the Marine
Corps and men in nursing—are cross-gender "freaks": masculine
women and feminine men.

To some extent, these two occupations themselves foster the
gender stereotypes. The Marine Corps actively promotes its image
as a proving ground for masculinity: Recruiters promise that the
military "will make a man out of you" and advertise that "the
Marine Corps is looking for a few good men." Likewise, nursing
has traditionally been promoted as a career for women—especially
single women—as preparation for motherhood. A 1943 advertisement for Cadet Schools of Nursing guaranteed to parents of future nurses that "when she marries, she'll be a better wife and

mother for the training she's getting now, and if she wants to stay in nursing after the war, it's a field in which a girl can go a long way."[1] Florence Nightingale, the founder of modern nursing, insisted on the close link between nursing and femininity as part of her effort to raise the status of nursing to a level suitable for ladies. Of all the nursing reforms instituted by Nightingale, this ideology of nursing as women's work has proved to be one of the most enduring.

The images of masculinity in the Marine Corps and femininity in nursing reflect the composition of the two organizations: 95.6 percent of all marines are men, and 97.3 percent of all nurses are women. In this regard, they are not unlike other highly sex-segregated occupations, which take on the "gendered" attributes associated with the sex of their work force. Secretaries (99 percent female), kindergarten and preschool teachers (98 percent female), and domestic workers (95 percent female) are all expected to be emotionally sensitive and nurturing, reflecting the "feminine" qualities of the workers.[2] Exhibiting stereotypically masculine qualities, engineers (96 percent male), airplane pilots (99 percent male), and auto mechanics (99 percent male) are assumed to be emotionally reserved and detached, concerned more with the rational manipulation of things than with the caring and support of people.

Although these cases seem extreme, they are merely exaggerated instances of a general social trend: the sexual segregation of work in American society. In 1980 almost half of all employed women worked in occupations that were at least 80 percent female, and more than two-thirds of all men were employed in occupations that were at least 80 percent male.[3] Most jobs in our economy are thought of as either "men's work" or "women's work." This assumption is so powerful that the few individuals of the "wrong" sex who cross over into highly sex-segregated occupations are commonly viewed as masculine women or feminine men. Think for a moment of the images that "male librarian" and "female truck driver" bring to mind.

But how accurate are these stereotypes? Despite their small numbers and the strong gender connotations of their occupations, female marines and male nurses do not conform to popular expectations. It is not unusual to hear it said that "Women Marines" are first and foremost "ladies"; nor is it unusual to hear male nurses characterized as strong, aggressive, or possessing leadership qualities.[4] Gender is actively constructed in these "nontraditional" occupations. Their very structure, as well as the efforts of their members, ensures that femininity is maintained in female marines and masculinity in male nurses.

Occupations foster gender differences among workers in a variety of ways, one of the most pervasive being "internal stratification." That is, men and women in the same occupation often perform different tasks and functions. A recent study of nearly four hundred firms found that most were either completely or nearly completely segregated by sex.[5] Even in those occupations that appear sexually integrated, the aggregate statistics often mask extreme internal segregation. Although the proportion of female bakers increased from 25 percent in 1970 to 41 percent in 1980, for example, the majority of female bakers are found in highly automated baking industries, while their male counterparts are located in less-automated bakeries. The same phenomenon has been detected among pharmacists, financial managers, and bus drivers— all groups where the influx of women workers suggests a diminution of sex segregation. But studies reveal that men and women usually perform different tasks and functions within these job categories.[6] The fact that the sexes rarely engage in the same activities on the job means that certain specialties can be feminine-identified and others masculine-identified—thus helping to preserve gender differences.

The Marine Corps and nursing are similarly segregated. In the Marine Corps, only 20 percent of the positions are even open to women.[7] Women are officially barred from any position that would directly involve them in combat. Consequently, female marines are overrepresented in traditionally "feminine" specialties—such as clerical work—that present no challenge to their feminine identity. In nursing, policy toward men is less clearly defined, yet in some parts of the country men are subject to restrictions on their training and choice of specialization. For example, some hospitals deny male nurses assignments to obstetrics and gynecology wards. By thus distinguishing "men's work" from "women's work," these occupations highlight and reproduce gender differences.

Another strategy used to maintain gender differences in supposedly integrated occupations is the use of sumptuary and etiquette rules. When women enter male-dominated occupations, certain rules are often introduced to govern their dress and demeanor. In office settings, for instance, dress codes—either formal or implicit—are not unusual; female employees may be required to wear dresses, nylons, and high-heeled shoes in order to enhance their femininity.[8] So it is for female marines and male nurses, both of whom are required to dress differently from their male and female counterparts. Male nurses never wear the traditional nursing cap; female marines never sport the standard Marine Corps garrison cap. Clothing differences are a constant symbolic reaffirmation of sex differences that accentuate the femininity of female marines and the masculinity of male nurses.

Informal practices also play a role in constituting femininity in female marines and masculinity in male nurses. As members of visible minority groups, they stand out at work and receive far more than their fair share of attention. This phenomenon was first documented by Rosabeth Moss Kanter, who found that women in corporations, simply by virtue of their numerical rarity, were noticed and scrutinized more than their male counterparts.[9] The fact that "numerically rare" men and women stand out this way can put added pressure on them in their jobs. A thirty-six-year-old master sergeant with sixteen and a half years of experience said this about being a woman in the Marine Corps:

> You're always on show. . . . Take myself and a male counterpart—
> same rank, same M.O.S. [military occupational specialty]—and

we're going into the same job. He's not going to have to prove himself at all, not one iota. He's going to be completely accepted until he messes up. I will not be accepted until I can prove that I can do the job better than he can.

This added pressure may actually result in different job performances from men and women in nontraditional occupations and exacerbate gender differences. Kanter's corporate women, for example, became more secretive, less independent, and less oppositional in response to their greater visibility—all traits that have traditionally been associated with femininity.[10]

Another informal technique that enhances gender differences is practiced by supervisors who evaluate men and women differently. The very qualities that are highly praised in one sex are sometimes denigrated in the other. Thus, a man is "ambitious," a woman, "pushy"; a woman is "sensitive," a man, "wimpy." Female marines and male nurses occasionally encounter such biased gender stereotypes from the people with whom they work. A nursing supervisor in a burn center reported: "At my last evaluation, my director admonished me not to be critical of my peers since I was 'a man, and have a natural advantage.' My director is female." Performance reports reveal similar "gender-based" biases against women in the air force. The following example illustrates the potentially damning effects of supervisors' assumptions about appropriate gender behavior: "Although she thinks like a man, she is always a lady and never too aggressive."[11] Even if the comment were intended as positive, this woman was probably judged less fit for higher rank than the men with whom she competed. Different expectations of men and women can unfairly advantage one group over another when promotion time rolls around—again enhancing the social differences between the sexes.

In each of these cases, gender differences are maintained through sexual segregation and discriminatory practices. Occupational segregation reinforces the belief that there are fundamental social and psychological differences between the sexes. Furthermore, because men and women in nontraditional occupations are treated differently from their peers of the opposite sex, they often behave differently.

But it would be a mistake to claim that all gender differences are forced on people. In addition to the external pressures I have just described, male nurses and female marines actively construct their own gender by redefining their activities in terms of traditional masculine and feminine traits. For example, women in the Marine Corps insist that their femininity is intact even as they march cadence in camouflage outfits. A twenty-year-old recruit told me, "We're equal with the men, but you can distinguish the difference. The men do it rough, and we do it rough, but we still have the feminine within ourselves. Appearance-wise. We do the same things the men do, but we're still women, 100 percent women." Likewise, male nurses contend that their masculinity is not at all threatened while they care for and nurture their patients. Both groups redefine femininity and masculinity in their daily lives, which also reinforces gender differences in these nontraditional contexts.

This "redefinition" is partly a response to the misgivings they encounter from people outside their occupations. Both male nurses and female marines report that outsiders often stereotype them as homosexual because of the preconception that male nurses are feminine and female marines, masculine. This assumption may drive men and women in these two occupations to conform even more closely to popular standards of the "appropriate" gender. Ironically, expressions of hyperfemininity among female marines and hypermasculinity among male nurses sometimes result.

The efforts of men and women in nontraditional occupations to vindicate and reassert their "true" gender identity, however, are not really different from the efforts of those of us in more "traditional" walks of life. The gendering process is simply more apparent for female marines and male nurses. For most people engaged in "traditional" activities, gender is still socially constructed and maintained, but in more subtle and less self-conscious ways.

Sigmund Freud wrote that "pathology, by making things larger and coarser, can draw our attention to normal conditions which would otherwise have escaped us."[12] In the study of gender, this tradition of exploring the "abnormal" to understand the "normal" has included such notable theorists as Harold Garfinkel and Robert Stoller, both of whom studied transsexuals to understand the social construction of gender in "normal" people.[13] Transsexuals—men and women who wish to be members of the opposite sex—must self-consciously construct their gender; they must learn what it means to be masculine and feminine and conform their behavior to these meanings in order to "pass" as a member of their desired sex. Theorists in this tradition contend that this is precisely what we all do, albeit much less self-consciously. It is easier for us to see what transsexuals do to make themselves thought of as males and females; their attempts at doing this, however, are only exaggerated versions of what all men and women do to maintain their gender identity. Transsexuals therefore constitute a fruitful beginning for a study of the "normal" process of gender construction and maintenance.

Similarly, female marines and male nurses, although they do not try to pass as members of the opposite sex, have their work cut out for them if they want to be considered "appropriately" gendered. The stereotype that male nurses are effeminate must somehow be counteracted during the course of the male nurse's day if he is to remain secure in his masculine identity. What he does to "vindicate" his masculinity is not unlike what men engaged in "masculine" activities do to prove that they are masculine—although the male nurse may be much more aware of what is at stake in his behavior. Female marines face the same task. Thus, by studying these two groups, we may gain some insight into the gendering process in general.

Official policies and informal practices, as well as the redefinition of work by men and women in nontraditional occupations, all function to maintain gender differences even when men and women are ostensibly engaged in the same occupation. This study explores in detail all these factors that enhance the femininity of women in the Marine Corps and the masculinity of men in nursing.

If we grant that masculinity and femininity persist in spite of men and women entering nontraditional occupations, a question still remains: *Why* is the maintenance of gender so important to people? In this book I not only document and describe *how* gender is reproduced in the occupational setting, but I also seek to explain *why* it is maintained. This would not have been considered a problem in the past, when biological sex differences were considered adequate explanations for all social differences between men and women. That is, if we believed that the female role in reproduction naturally predisposed women to display the nurturant, passive qualities we associate with femininity, the persistence of femininity in women in the Marine Corps wouldn't surprise us. However, most sociologists and psychologists now recognize a basic distinction between biological sex and gender. "Sex" refers to the different primary and secondary reproductive characteristics that men and women are born with (or develop), and "gender" refers to the social, cultural, and psychological meanings, practices, and organizational arrangements associated with those differences. The central premise of the sociology of gender is that biological and anatomical sex differences are meaningless outside of a social context. That is, the various meanings and practices associated with sex differences are socially constituted, not biologically given. Information about chromosomes and reproductive organs will not help us understand why female marines are feminine and male nurses are masculine.

An alternative approach to this question of *why* gender is maintained in nontraditional occupations is to examine the specific interests served by doing so: Who benefits from maintaining femininity in female marines and masculinity in male nurses? In fact, men in both groups—male marines and male nurses—benefit from the perpetuation of gender because our society has traditionally rewarded masculine qualities more highly than feminine qualities. It avails men to monopolize masculine qualities, emphasize them in themselves, and enforce femininity on their female counterparts.[14] Thus, by insisting that women are unsuited for certain military assignments (e.g., combat billets), men in the Marine Corps reserve the highest paying and most prestigious jobs for themselves. Likewise in nursing, because male nurses are assumed to be more career-minded, aggressive, and demanding than their female colleagues, they are often channeled into the more prestigious and better paying administrative and leadership positions. Thus, a fundamental asymmetry in the economic consequences of "gender maintenance" for men and women in these two nontraditional occupations works out to the benefit of men.

Over the past twenty years, radical and socialist feminists have focused sociologists' attention on the coercive nature of gender arrangements. Heidi Hartmann, for example, has argued that men in our society dominate and oppress women out of a power-seeking drive to control resources and to gain important household services that they themselves do not wish to perform: "[Men's] control of women's labor power is the lever that allows men to benefit from women's provision of personal and household services, including relief from childrearing and many unpleasant tasks both within and beyond households."[15] Many feminists point out that it is in the rational self-interest of the dominant group in society (men) to allocate such tasks to women.[16]

Important factor though it is, economic self-interest alone does not adequately account for the maintenance of gender in nursing and the Marine Corps; preserving it serves irrational needs as well. Clues to these largely subterranean forces surface in spirited diatribes against integration:

> War is man's work. Biological convergence on the battlefield would not only be dissatisfying in terms of what women could do, but it would be an enormous psychological distraction for the male who wants to think that he's fighting for that woman somewhere behind, not up there in the same foxhole with him. It tramples the male ego. When you get right down to it, you have to protect the

manliness of war. [General William Barrows, former Marine Corps
commandant][17]

The perpetuation of gender in nontraditional occupations serves
both men's emotional and their economic interests.

In fact, I have found that men in both the Marine Corps and
the nursing profession do make greater efforts than women to
distinguish their roles from those performed by the opposite sex.
For example, male nurses contend that although they care for
patients, their caring is provided in a characteristically "masculine"
sort of way. One male nurse told me:

> I think men demonstrate nurturance and caring to the same degree
> as a female would, but the demonstration of it is different. I don't
> think we always touch as frequently, and say soft, kind words. I
> think my caring is of the same depth and degree, but it's more overt
> than covert. It's not warm fluffy; it's different. Some might say
> that's not caring or nurturing.

Likewise, male soldiers distance themselves from their female
counterparts, insisting that women are incapable of achieving full-
fledged membership in the Marine Corps. But unlike men in
nursing, men in the military can deny women full active participation and segregate them into certain specialties because they monopolize positions of authority and set official policy. Thus, in the
Marine Corps women are excluded from participating in certain
occupational specialties, they are segregated in basic training, and
they are subject to all sorts of rules about personal conduct and
bearing that are not applied to men.

Women, however, seek to minimize the role differences between themselves and their male colleagues. Female marines un-
derplay the importance of sex differences in job performance, for
the most part insisting that they are as capable as men of carrying
out their duties. One recruit, lamenting the unequal treatment of
men and women in training, told me, "I don't see why the men
should get more training than we get. I think it should be straight
down the line equal. Women shouldn't be kept out of combat. I

definitely would go! If a woman really wants it, I think it should be open. I think it's the policymakers that keep us from entering combat; not the women themselves." Like most of the recruits I interviewed, this young woman expressed no trepidation about engaging in quintessentially masculine pursuits. Even the possibility of armed combat alongside men posed no essential challenge to her self-identity as a female. Unlike men's masculinity, women's femininity does not seem to be threatened when they engage in nontraditional activities.

In order to understand how these different emotional interests evolved—why men seem to have more at stake emotionally than women in preserving and maintaining gender differences—we must examine the socialization process. From the moment we place male infants in blue blankets and females in pink ones, we create two classes of humans with different emotional needs that stay with them throughout adulthood. For example, studies have found that parents caress and hold infant daughters more frequently than sons, which may create in women a greater desire and need for emotional intimacy.[18] Thus, if we explore the constitution of gender in childhood, we can gain some insight into the different emotional needs and dispositions found among adult men and women—including insight into men's greater need for maintaining gender differences.

There are several theories of gender formation and maintenance, the most popular of which may be sex role theory.[19] Talcott Parsons, perhaps the "founding father" of this theory, maintained that differentiated male and female roles are functional, or stabilizing forces for both the family and the rest of society.[20] He argued that society, not biology, dictates that men and women develop different personality traits and assume different roles. The men produced by sex role socialization are well adapted to the achievement-oriented, instrumental demands of the occupational world. Properly socialized women are able to fulfill the "expressive" needs of society: They learn the care-giving skills that are essential both for child rearing and for comforting fatigued husbands after their exhausting days of instrumental labor. The roles are thus complementary; they are equally necessary to ensure the smooth operation of society.

In general, then, the sex role perspective focuses on how boys and girls learn to conform to society's expectations about sex-specific activities, norms, and attitudes. Parents, teachers, peers, television, and various other socializing agents teach children which roles are feminine and which are masculine. By the time they are adults, they have been exposed to sufficient formal and informal "role training," or conditioning, to make them properly socialized individuals ready, able, and for the most part willing to assume their appropriate—and complementary—roles.

Even though sex role theory emphasizes social rather than biological determinants of gender differences, it suffers from one major drawback: neglect of the myriad variations in the meanings individuals attach to their social activities. The theory focuses on behavioral conformity to static sex roles rather than on the processes whereby individuals actively construct definitions of masculinity and femininity. As a consequence, the theory simply cannot account for masculine male nurses or feminine female marines. From this perspective, individuals entering these occupations would be expected to conform to the gender characteristics associated with these fields. Women in the Marine Corps would be expected to possess the "masculine," aggressive qualities associated with soldiering, and male nurses would be expected to be "feminine" (e.g., caring and passive).

Psychoanalytic theory, with its more "dynamic" approach to gender formation and maintenance, offers an alternative approach to the gender socialization process.[21] It recognizes that socialization is not a one-way street. Individuals bring to every social interaction a particular set of motives, interests, and desires not entirely reducible to contemporary social forces. The forms of social interaction are not standardized and independent of their particular manifestations in real people; they constantly change, depending upon the actors' dispositions. Individuals do not simply conform to preset "roles"; they bring their own interests and desires to bear upon their social activities, often redefining them in the process.

This does not mean, however, that we cannot generalize about human social behavior. Sociologists writing within the psychoanalytic framework argue that social arrangements—particularly family structure—channel individual desire in certain directions. Nancy Chodorow has been the single most influential theorist on this process in recent years.[22] She argues that boys' and girls' earliest relationships to their mothers result in different unconscious emotional needs in adult men and women. Because in our society women typically are in charge of child care, especially that of infants, the first emotional tie for both sexes is to a woman. This means, in psychoanalytic parlance, that everyone is originally "feminine-identified." This identification makes gender a problematic issue for males: Boys face substantial pressures to deny their early attachment when it comes time for them to assume a masculine gender identity. Chodorow writes: "A boy, in order to feel himself adequately masculine, must distinguish and differentiate himself from others in a way that a girl need not—must categorize himself as someone apart. Moreover, he defines masculinity negatively as that which is not feminine."[23] The assumption of masculinity is predicated on the denial and repression of early feminine attachments. The assumption of a feminine gender continues the woman's earliest identification with her mother.

Robert Stoller, who has studied gender disorders in men and women, describes in detail the conflict males experience over establishing masculinity. He, too, notes that during infancy both boys and girls are "merged" with their mothers; they actually sense themselves as "part" of her. This symbiosis, according to Stoller, establishes a sense of femininity in *all* infants, thus promising an eventual problem for males, who have to renounce this identification later in life. He writes:

I suspect that the problem boys have with creating their masculinity from the protofemininity leaves behind a "structure," a vigilance, a fear of the pull of the symbiosis—that is, a conflict between the urge to return to the peace of the symbiosis and the opposing urge to separate out as an individual, as a male, as masculine. . . . Much of what we see as masculinity is, I think, the effect of that struggle. For much of masculinity, as is well known, consists of struggling not to be seen by oneself or others as having feminine attributes, physical or psychologic. One must maintain one's distance from women or be irreparably infected with femininity.[24]

Girls fare much better in establishing their adult gender identity. Because they are feminine-identified from the start, they have a developmental advantage over boys. Stoller writes that because the girl's first love object is female, "the development of her femininity no longer seems so risk laden. Those conflict-free aspects of gender identity (for example, those that result from identifying with the gratifying aspects of being a woman) are present from earliest life."[25] Adult men are more concerned than women with establishing and defending their gender identity because of their different early ties to their mothers.

This description of adult men constantly worrying about the viability of their masculinity while women seem relatively unconcerned about maintaining their femininity is precisely what I observed among male nurses and female marines. In fact, the psychic dispositions psychoanalysts describe are practically caricatured in these two groups. Male nurses go to great lengths to carve for themselves a special niche within nursing that they then define as masculine; preserving their masculinity *requires* distancing themselves from women. Women in the Marine Corps feel they could maintain their femininity even in a foxhole alongside the male "grunts." For the women I interviewed, femininity was not "role defined" in the way that masculinity was for the male nurses. It mattered little what activity she was engaged in; a woman in the Marine Corps could be employed in *any* job specialty and still be considered a "lady" by her female peers. This asymmetry in the meaning of gender for men and women in nontraditional occupations derives from the asymmetry in their early childhood experience. These two groups thus provide remarkably rich illustrations of the adult consequences of our gender socialization process.

Psychoanalysis offers a vivid and compelling explanation of why gender is such a salient issue in these two occupations. It uncovers hidden motives and unconscious desires behind efforts to preserve female marines' femininity and male nurses' masculinity. However, obtaining data on psychological processes is difficult, if not impossible, outside of a clinical setting. I conducted one-time in-depth interviews with male nurses and female marines. This type of data cannot inform questions about infantile identifications, castration anxiety, or penis envy; only psychoanalysis itself can tap into these deep psychological processes. My observations and discussions with male nurses and female marines cannot, therefore, be construed as offering "proof" of psychoanalytic insights. But my interviews do illustrate how the conflicts that psychoanalysts associate with gender identity development may manifest themselves in adult life. The chapters that follow describe in some detail this "match" between the experiences of male nurses and female marines and the psychoanalytic analysis of gender.

At the start of my project, I spoke to the directors of the ROTC (Reserve Officers Training Command) department at the University of California, Berkeley. They were extremely enthusiastic about my project and put me in contact with women naval ROTC students (whom I subsequently surveyed), several high-ranking female officers in the Bay Area, and a representative of the Defense Advisory Committee on Women in the Services (DACOWITS), a civilian organization that advises the Department of Defense. From there my contacts reached all the way to the Pentagon. The Washington, D.C., staff of DACOWITS arranged interviews with high-ranking military policymakers on the topic of women's integration into the military.

Meanwhile, I learned of the existence of a veterans' organization for female marines: the Women Marines Association (WMA). I contacted its leaders, who invited me to their 1984 biannual convention in Indiana. I described my research to the two hundred convention attendees and had the opportunity to conduct several in-depth interviews with World War II veterans. I also distributed a short, open-ended questionnaire to the participants.

At the convention I met an active duty Woman Marine who worked in the public relations office of the Marine Corps Training Depot at Parris Island, South Carolina, the only place in the country where women recruits are trained. She encouraged me to write to her supervisor and request to study women recruit training. I did so, and I was immediately invited to visit the Parris Island Depot. During my two weeks there (in April 1985), I spent between eight and ten hours at the depot every day. I was assigned an assistant (a Woman Marine staff sergeant) who became a key informant and helped me set up interviews with recruits, drill instructors, and women working at other locations on the depot. I was given complete freedom in selecting my subjects. While I was there, I was taken on several guided tours of Parris Island and observed physical and field training of men and women recruits. I also participated in one of the most challenging aspects of training: rappelling off a forty-five-foot tower.

In 1985 I also visited an air force base in the southwestern part of the country. I contacted the Equal Opportunity Office of the base and was granted permission to interview female instructor pilots and women in pilot training.

I conducted sixty-eight formal interviews of women in the military, including twenty-one formal interviews with Women Marine recruits, fourteen with Women Marine drill instructors, three with Women Marine officers, and ten with Women Marine veterans of World War II. I also conducted six interviews with military men (enlisted and officer), eight with female officers from branches of the military other than the Marine Corps, and six interviews with Pentagon officials. In addition, I talked informally about my research questions to dozens of people while I was at the WMA convention and at Parris Island (on the drill field, at the rappelling tower, and in the "D.I. huts," the offices used by active drill instructors).

I received forty-six returns (out of approximately two hundred distributed) from my survey questionnaire handed out at the WMA convention and six returns (out of twelve distributed) from my ROTC survey of naval cadets.

Studying men in nursing proved to be more difficult than studying women in the Marine Corps. In order to develop contacts, I had hoped to have access to nursing directories kept by the regional nursing associations. However, my requests for this access were denied. As a result, I relied on "snowball" techniques for developing my sample.

I first contacted male professors of nursing from baccalaureate programs of nursing listed in college bulletins. The professors who responded to my request for interviews put me in contact with nursing student leaders, who in turn introduced me to fellow male students.

I also wanted to interview men not connected to nursing education. Through friends and colleagues I was introduced to female nurses, who then put me in contact with their male colleagues. This was a slow process: Each female nurse I interviewed typically knew only one male nurse to whom she could refer me.

I was unable to contact male nurses through more systematic means. One nurse I interviewed did volunteer to give me a list of his male colleagues in a large metropolitan hospital. He also gave me the name of the personnel director at his hospital, expecting that she could help me establish contacts. However, when I contacted her, she informed me that I could not interview any nurses at the hospital without obtaining the approval of their internal human subjects protection committee, a process she said took up to six months. Furthermore, she denied me permission to call the nurses at work without prior committee approval. My previous contact was either unwilling or unable to give me the home phone

numbers of his colleagues. Suspecting that his reluctance was motivated in part by the personnel director's resistance, I did not press
him for further contacts.

My final source of informants was the membership of a national male nurses' organization, the American Assembly for Men
in Nursing (AAMN). When I contacted this organization with a
request for bibliographic information, their support was enthusiastic. They invited me to attend their annual meeting in Chicago in
1985 and in Indianapolis in 1986, where I had the opportunity to
interview dozens of men in nursing from all over the country and
to distribute an open-ended questionnaire. Subsequently, I have
presented portions of my research findings to a local chapter of
this organization and have received valuable feedback.

In sum, I conducted twenty-five formal in-depth interviews
with male nurses. I also interviewed five female nurses. I received
twenty-seven returns (out of approximately a hundred distributed) of my open-ended survey.

My different experiences conducting research in the military
and nursing tempt me to draw some general preliminary contrasts
between the status of men and women in these two occupations.
The military was eager to demonstrate to me how well women are
progressing in this formerly all-male preserve. On the whole, the
military policymakers are tremendously proud of the strides they
believe women have made in every branch of the service. The
military people I contacted went out of their way to accommodate
all my requests for interviews and data.

The situation with nursing was quite the reverse. The men's
organization was the only source of support approximating my
enthusiastic reception by the military. Yet in the nurses' case (unlike the marines' case) I felt their support was tied to the men's
desire to "expose" discrimination in their treatment by the nursing
profession. The marines seemed to have no such agenda.

These observations could be attributable to any number of
extraneous factors that have nothing to do with gender. However,
it is interesting to note these differences in the context of my

study's findings. Women continue to be subject to widespread discriminatory policies and practices that severely limit their participation in the military. Men in nursing, however, experience few such barriers and are not generally subject to informal discrimination. The question whether men and women perceive discrimination differently therefore arises. The "special treatment" accorded to female marines was generally considered unproblematic and beyond reproach by the "gatekeepers" and my informants in the military. Yet the mere *potential* for discrimination in the treatment of male nurses made the entire topic a sensitive one for the "gatekeepers" and my informants in nursing. This is but one of the several asymmetries I discovered in the social construction and maintenance of gender in female marines and male nurses.

My concluding chapter provides an in-depth analysis of these asymmetries. Chapters Three and Four document and describe the treatment of women in the military and men in nursing. Chapter Two reviews the history of the sexual integration of these two occupations. World War II stands as a watershed period for both women in the military and men in nursing. During this period both groups struggled for public acceptance and recognition, with different degrees of success. The efforts to integrate these two occupations during World War II sheds light on some of the ways that gender is socially constructed and maintained. Then, as now, much of the debate over integration was waged on ideological terrain: Are men capable of caring for other men? Will the presence of women in uniform threaten the morale of fighting soldiers? In fact, all the debates revolved around the question of acceptable gender behavior. Understanding what was at stake in those debates provides the groundwork for examining the persistence of sexual stratification in these occupations today.

2

Integrating the Marine Corps and Nursing

Until quite recently the military has been virtually an all-male preserve, with women serving only in nominal strengths prior to 1973.[1] During World War II, however, there was a surge of female enlistments: Three hundred fifty thousand women served in the women's reserves of the army, navy, and marines, and another 64,000 women joined the Army and Navy Nursing Corps. This represented 2 percent of the total forces, then the largest percentage of women ever to serve in the history of the U.S. military. The majority of these women filled clerical and administrative positions—long considered women's traditional domain. Yet thousands were trained in aviation mechanics, parachute packing, motor transport, and other specialties that had previously been the sole purview of male soldiers.

Women and men were often engaged in identical tasks, but official military policy and the dominant ideology of gender perpetuated the division of labor by sex. Thus, women's nontraditional activities were interpreted in ways that supported a traditional sex role arrangement. This meant that women could maintain their femininity in spite of the military's traditional identification as a masculine occupation.

Only a few military women ever assumed leadership or policy-making positions during World War II; this power was almost exclusively in the hands of white men, who had almost total power to define and enforce the parameters of what they considered "appropriate" female behavior. How the ideology of femininity was then construed reflects both the material and the emotional interests of these men.

In this chapter I examine the constraints placed on the women who served in World War II, in both the reserves and the nursing corps. I show how the maintenance of a specific ideology of femininity was a top priority of policymakers and how this "femininity maintenance" prevented any challenge to the sexual segregation of the military work force. I also describe the reactions of a group of World War II Woman Marine veterans to the de facto segregation of their military work and explore some of the reasons women did not resist the exclusionary policies that had governed them during their enlistments. Finally, I examine the attempted integration of men into the all-female military nursing corps. Military policymakers maintained both masculinity and femininity. The challenge to sexual segregation by male nurses reveals how formidable the ideology of gender can be.

WOMEN IN THE MILITARY RESERVES

In order to qualify for the auxiliaries, a woman had to be between twenty-one and thirty-six (under forty-four for the Women's Auxiliary Army Corps, the predecessor of the Women's Army Corps), white (except for the WAAC, which permitted 10 percent of its members to be black—although they were never more than 6 percent), and without dependent children. The women who joined the services during World War II enlisted "for the duration"; they did not have the option of continuing careers in the military. The female directors of the four branches of the service defended this policy. The director of the Marine Corps Women's Reserve wanted to disband the reserves after the war reportedly because "the type of woman who would volunteer after the passage of the GI Bill would be motivated by self-interest instead of patriotism."² General G. C. Thomas, Marine Corps director of plans and policies, elaborated:

> The opinion generally held by the Marine Corps is that women have no proper place or function in the regular service in peacetime. The American tradition is that a woman's place is in the home. . . . Women do not take kindly to military regimentation. During the war they have accepted the regulations imposed on them, but hereafter the problem of enforcing discipline alone would be a headache.³

General Eisenhower, one of the biggest supporters of the WAC, concurred: He predicted that "after an enlistment or two enlistments women will ordinarily—and thank God—they will get married."⁴

Thus, women were allowed to enter the military during wartime only as a temporary emergency measure. Military leaders viewed their contributions as supporting the men who served: The women's branches were, after all, called "auxiliaries." Policymakers insisted that this status corresponded to women's motivations for joining the services. Women, they believed, did not join for selfish reasons (e.g., lure of adventure and a well-paying job), but rather to care for and support the fighting men. Thus, they attributed "feminine" motivations for what would otherwise have been considered a masculine calling.

Marriage and pregnancy were issues of major concern for War Department policymakers. The War Department originally wanted only single women to be allowed to join up, but this turned out to be unrealistic given recruitment needs. Ultimately, a married woman could enlist if her husband wasn't in the service she chose to join. Officially, the main reason for the exclusion of married women was the military's rule against fraternization between officers and enlisted personnel. Most of the enlisted women had characteristics similar to those of officers (e.g., some college education, middle-class backgrounds), so married partners in the same branch would have frequently found each other on different sides of the enlisted/officer divide—which would have made for unacceptable living arrangements. If two members of the same branch married while on active duty, the couple was split up and stationed at "widely separate posts," or the woman was forced to resign.⁵ Many couples averted this possibility by simply not marrying and, as a military chaplain at the time complained, instead lived together in "a condition of concubinage."

The reluctance to enlist married women was also based on policymakers' fears that married women's loyalties would be divided between their husbands and the military. Thus, the marines abandoned a plan to allow wives of marine prisoners of war and soldiers missing in action to enlist because "many felt that when the men returned the women would quit."⁶

Policymakers all agreed that pregnancy had no place in the military; it was grounds for discharge from all the services.⁷ In addition, if a woman was suspected of having had an abortion, she could be discharged on the grounds of misconduct. (Prior to World War II both marriage and pregnancy were grounds for *dishonorable* discharge for women serving in the Army Nurse Corps.)

The military policymakers thus demonstrated a strong ambivalence about enlisting women. On the one hand, they believed that the only legitimate reasons for women to serve were traditionally feminine ones (i.e., to help out the fighting men). On the other hand, any manifestation of the traditional feminine role outside of the military (marriage, family, pregnancy) was sternly frowned upon.

Black women faced an even more formidable double bind in the services. Only the army's auxiliary permitted black women to join, and they were segregated into separate platoons in basic training and served mainly on posts with large numbers of black servicemen. Officially, this was because "it was deemed most desirable for adjustment to assign units to posts where a number of Negro troops were stationed, or where there was a large Negro population in nearby cities."⁸ However, a story told by Treadwell, the official historian of the Women's Army Corps, reveals the policymakers' real intentions: "The inspector general at Sioux Falls suggested that large groups of Negro W.A.C.'s be brought by truck from Des Moines to make up for the recreational deficiencies of Negro men at that air base."⁹ Because policymakers cast women in a feminine support role, it is not surprising that the general assumed this role should carry into the *private* lives of the servicemen.

Given racial segregation, and the belief that women's role was to "free a man to fight," the only acceptable justification for enlisting a black woman was to free a black man to fight. This is precisely how the then secretary of the navy defended the exclusion of black women from the WAVES (Women Accepted for Volunteer Emergency Service, the navy women's auxiliary):

> Since the Navy "lacked any substantial body of colored men available or qualified for general service at sea" there was no need for women to relieve black sailors on land, which was the primary task of the WAVES. Asked whether black women might not relieve landlocked navy men of any color in non-combat jobs, the Secretary simply replied "no."¹⁰

Thus, in this case military enforcement of gender and racist exclusionary policies reinforced one another.

The War Department's campaigns to recruit women into the services shed more light on the significance of this historic first for women. Women's role in the military was construed as support in a temporary emergency, and the most popular campaign slogan was "free a man to fight." One poster aimed at getting this message across portrayed a frustrated serviceman literally chained to a desk and typewriter, gazing at a poster of a soldier on his way to the front. This image was a blatant appeal to the division of labor between the sexes and offered no challenge to the stratification system that had excluded women from participating in the military until then.

But the interpretation of women's contribution as auxiliary to the war effort was not limited to those doing clerical work.

Women's participation even in the nontraditional mechanical and technical fields that they entered in overwhelming numbers was couched in the framework of support for the fighting men.

Throughout the war, the types of jobs women were permitted to hold were reevaluated. Those previously considered "masculine" were redefined as "feminine." Women who entered occupations previously closed to them were not seen as challenging sexual stereotypes: In fact, the work they did was restereotyped as "feminine." Ruth Milkman has shown how this phenomenon operated in the civilian world in her study of the auto and electronics industries in World War II:

> Rather than hiring women workers to fill openings as vacancies occurred, managers explicitly defined some war jobs as "suitable" for women, and others as "unsuitable," guided by a hastily revised idiom of sex-typing that adapted prewar traditions to the special demands of the war emergency. . . . Wartime propaganda imagery of "woman's place" on the nation's production lines consistently portrayed women's war work as a temporary extension of domesticity. And jobs that had previously been viewed as quintessentially masculine were suddenly endowed with femininity and glamour for the duration.[11]

The same qualities that suited women to perform household duties were suddenly the very ones needed to operate the heavy machinery in defense plants!

Milkman argues that the wartime sexual division of labor was largely the result of management's efforts to fill opening factory positions with women in a way that would not threaten to undermine the traditional division of labor and the temporary nature of women's commitment to the paid labor force. This would permit employers to reassign the men to their previous jobs once the war was over.

The situation of women in the military was in many ways similar. When the bill to form a woman's auxiliary in the military was first introduced in 1941, its mission was clearly stated: The WAAC was established "for the purpose of making available to the national defense the knowledge, skill, and special training of the women of the nation."[12] The early goal of the women's corps was not to free up manpower for combat, but rather to provide a small, elite, highly educated corps of women with special technical skills that men could not generally be expected to possess. The army thought it much more prudent to hire women typists, for example, than to spend extra time and resources training men to type. Military planners insisted that "both educational and technical qualifications should be set exceptionally high to make of the projected organization an elite corps, in order that it may quickly attain the highest reputation for both character and professional excellence."[13] However, these same planners who insisted on such high educational and moral standards also specified the jobs of charwoman and laundry worker as appropriate tasks for the new women's corps.

As the war progressed and manpower shortages were more keenly felt, increasing numbers of military jobs opened up to women. A 1942 War Department study indicated that women could perform as many as two-thirds of all jobs in the services. Remaining closed to them were combat billets, jobs requiring considerable physical strength, jobs that entailed supervisorial command over men, and "jobs requiring that personnel be engaged at particularly unfavorable hours." Tasks considered most appropriate for women included "all clerical jobs, especially those involving typing or requiring fairly routine tasks but coupled with a high degree of accuracy in the work." Other mechanical and technical positions (e.g., repairing fire control instruments) were opened for women purportedly because of their greater "finger dexterity."[14]

In December 1942, the Antiaircraft Artillery (AAA) units in Washington, D.C., and four other major U.S. cities undertook a top-secret experiment: Women were integrated into combat batteries. Their jobs included operating tactical machinery and instruments and performing clerical duties. They were barred from actually firing weapons, and they were not assigned to outlying searchlight positions "because of the isolation and the fact that the public would have observed the experiment."[15] The women performed quite well, as the following excerpt from the final report to the War Department by those in charge of the "experiment" shows:

> WAAC personnel can be used in performing many of the tasks of the Antiaircraft Artillery. They are superior to men in all functions involving delicacy of manual dexterity, such as operation at the director, height finder, radar, and searchlight control systems. They perform routine repetitious tasks in a manner superior to men. . . . The morale of women used in the AAA was generally high due to the fact that they felt that they were making a direct contribution to the successful prosecution of the war.[16]

However, the success of "integration" should be taken with a grain of salt for two reasons. First, real integration clearly did not take place. Not only were the women segregated into specific duties, but their performance evaluations reflect preconceived and limited expectations of their abilities. Second, the plan to employ women in the AAA was dropped! General G. C. Marshall, the original instigator of the experiment, decided that "national policy or public opinion [was not] yet ready to accept the use of women in field force units [and that such use was not] presently necessary."[17] Thus, despite the fact that the AAA requisitioned the appointment of 2,418 WAAC soldiers, the issue was discretely shelved.

De facto segregation of jobs by sex in the military contributed to the maintenance of traditional gender norms by encouraging both men and women to distinguish between the contributions each could and should make to the war effort. In addition, the temporary and auxiliary nature of women's participation in the military was constantly reiterated by wartime propaganda, reflecting policymakers' concern with maintaining the traditional conceptions of sex roles. A particularly telling recruitment poster for the U.S. Marine Corps urged women to "become a marine—free a marine to fight!" The ambiguous use of the word "marine" underscores women's ambiguous position in the corps. Although performing most of the jobs held by men, they weren't really marines, a status reserved for those able to be positioned on the battlefield (male marines). No one ever questioned the full marine status of the men who worked beside the women (although half of all military personnel never left the states, and only one-eighth actually saw combat).[18]

Both the official policies and the propaganda literature of World War II thus undermined the potential for restructuring the sexual division of labor after the war. Women's participation in fields that had previously excluded them on the basis of sex was couched in terms of traditional support for the men in a manner that did not challenge women's primary responsibilities to the home and family. Ironically, women's war work—as mediated by official policy and propaganda—actually promoted feminine stereotypes.

THE WOMEN WHO SERVED

To what extent did the women themselves feel like temporary workers contributing their feminine skills to a moral cause? Did they object to the special treatment they were subject to?

In 1984 I attended a convention of the Women Marines Association, a veterans' organization whose members include women who served in the Marine Corps Women's Reserve in World War II. There I conducted approximately thirty informal interviews and surveyed a sample of forty-five Women Marines.

Although it would be impossible to determine what actually motivated women to join the services, my interviews confirmed the results of a more systematic survey on this topic conducted by the Marine Corps during the war. Recognizing that patriotism was by far the most frequently reported reason for joining during the war, the Marine Corps asked, "What was the *next* most important reason you joined?" Some 25 percent of the women said they joined to escape either a bad job or a bad family situation, 35 percent said they did it because they had male relatives in the service, 6 percent joined because they had no relatives in the service, and 4 percent enlisted because members of their family had been killed while in the service. Another 30 percent enlisted either for adventure or for the material benefits of military life.[19]

The Women Marines I surveyed held very strong opinions about sexual equality. They felt that men and women should be given equal opportunity to engage in every military occupational specialty (MOS), with the unanimous exception of hand-to-hand combat. These are comments from two female veterans:

> I believe in equal pay for equal work. . . . Intellectually, women are equal to men, but physically *most* men are stronger. A large percentage of being a marine is physical. I personally could not endure 1984 boot camp on an equal basis. (I can't remember if I would have been able forty years ago. I'm sixty-five years old now.) There are women in their twenties who are physically and mentally capable. They should be given a chance, an *honest* chance. . . . It's worth a good try, if a gal wants it.

> I believe if a woman is equally qualified in, say, airplane mechanics, she should be able to work side by side with a man and possibly be in command. I feel that fighting side by side with a gun or sharing a trench, or hand-to-hand combat is not quite what I'd like to see our Women Marines do. Yet women pilots are good as men if not better. My vision of seeing a woman in aerial combat is something that is awesome to me.

The Marine Corps has always segregated men and women in basic training and has required higher standards for enlistment for women. Although the World War II Women Marines felt strongly about equal opportunity, most were decidedly not in favor of integrating the sexes in training:

> Women have a definite place in the military, just as men do. But I certainly do not feel that women belong in combat, nor should they be quartered in the same barracks, or expected to eat the same food. Just the food issue alone: Sometimes in my service, I had to use the men's mess halls. At times I chose not to eat, at all, because the food was so heavy, greasy, and unappealing. Especially when piled on a metal tray, with everything mixed up—at that point it wasn't food, it became garbage. . . . Horrible![20]

When I asked forty-five women veterans of World War II on a written survey, "What were your major concerns (if any) at the time you enlisted about being a woman in the Marine Corps," most insisted that they had none, others wrote that physically making it through boot camp was their greatest worry, and still others said they had been apprehensive about how well they would be accepted by male marines. A former private first class who worked in aviation parts supply summed up the worries of many of her contemporaries: "[I worried] if I was physically able to take boot camp. If I was mentally able to take the harassment from the men. How the men would accept us and if I could adjust to wearing nothing but a uniform for the duration (no civies allowed during the war)." Another woman wrote: "I worried a little that people out of the service might not think of us as feminine." These women did not perceive that their feminine identity was incompatible with service in the Marine Corps, but some did worry that others might believe that it was. In fact, the women I spoke to did not attempt to recast their wartime duty in a "feminine" light. They apparently did not need to justify their Marine Corps experience as compatible with traditional feminine roles. None of the women I met even considered the possibility that the Marine Corps might not be an appropriate place for women.

Two distinct conclusions could be drawn from this. On the one hand, the fact that women saw nothing incompatible with their wartime service and their feminine identity could mean that the wartime propaganda that redefined women's new roles as "feminine" was eminently successful. Why should women worry about their femininity? They were, after all, constantly being reassured that what they were doing was feminine, temporary, and auxiliary to fighting the war.

But another conclusion may be warranted instead: Perhaps women didn't need the reassurances that what they were doing was feminine because engaging in nontraditional work did not threaten their feminine identity. The women I interviewed did not justify their wartime contribution in terms of "feminine support."

Some were actually insulted by the suggestion that their work was auxiliary to the war effort or that what they were doing was in any way different from what had been done by the men they replaced. The women, it seems to me, would have enlisted whether or not efforts had been made to convince them they could join the military without undermining their femininity.

I believe that the military's efforts to preserve female reserves' femininity were meant to assuage the trepidations of the *men* in the military, not the women. Men were threatened by the idea that women could replace them at their archetypically "masculine" occupation. They—rather than the women—needed to be convinced that military women were still feminine.

A malicious "slander campaign" directed against all the women's auxiliaries expressed the threats created by women in uniform. Widespread rumors circulated that they were either prostitutes or lesbians.[21] The War Department took these rumors quite seriously because they came at a time (1943) when the services were all attempting to recruit more women to fill "manpower" shortages. The War Department went so far in its investigation as to bring in the FBI to discern whether the slander campaign was an Axis plot to break down soldier morale and military strength.

The results of the exhaustive FBI investigation are extremely revealing: "Evidence indicated that in most cases the obscene stories had been originated by the men of the armed forces at about the time of the change from the 'phony war' to real combat in North Africa, and of Congressional publicity on the thousands of women sought to release men for combat."[22] Furthermore, military intelligence agencies found that "enlisted male attitudes were the most important impediment to hesitant female prospects."[23] The very men the women were supposedly there to "support" had initiated the foul rumors about them. I believe there were two reasons for this. On the one hand, many men resented the possibility of losing their desk jobs and being sent off to combat; many did not want women to "free" them to fight. Yet the intensity of the malicious rumors suggests a deeper underlying motivation:

The integration of women into the military threatened not only their jobs but their masculinity.

Psychoanalytic theory argues that masculinity, unlike femininity, is an achieved identity. Men who are successful in the military have, in a sense, *proven* their masculinity because the military is so closely associated with masculine identity. However, this sense of achievement diminished drastically once women were allowed to join the group. The backlash against women in uniform reaffirmed the masculine essence of the military: If some women could make it as marines, the men concluded, there must be something unfeminine about those women. The only other viable conclusion would have been that there is nothing inherently masculine about military service—clearly an unacceptable idea to those who have struggled to "make the grade."

The women eventually became quite defensive about the affronts to their femininity. For example, a group of Women Marines told me a story about a woman in their company who was discharged for pregnancy. The commander called the entire company into formation in front of the mess hall, where the pregnant woman was physically stripped of her stripes, insignia, and buttons in a humiliating display. Everyone was mortified—but not because they felt the punishment was unjust. To them, she deserved this treatment because she had brought shame to them by feeding the gossip mills with her lack of precaution. They explained that they all had encountered negative stereotypes from both civilian and Marine Corps men that Women Marines were wild women, "playthings for the men." This put pressure on them to maintain a stellar image at all times. The Women Marines perceived correctly that any individual's behavior that could be construed negatively would be taken by the men as representative of the behavior of all women in the services. Even though they realized that the bad reputations they had were constructed by the men and didn't match reality, they understood that they were on trial, charged with not maintaining appropriate feminine behavior.

Approximately half of the discharged servicewomen joined the civilian labor force immediately after the war (although 89 percent had been employed prior to enlisting). Only 22 percent returned to their former jobs (compared with twice that percentage of returning servicemen who went back to their prewar jobs). The overwhelming majority of female veterans did not use the new skills they had learned during their enlistments; only two in five employed women were able to use their new skills on the job after the war.[24] In fact, many who had received special training in mechanics or avionics contended that these skills were actually deterrents to getting any job. The male veterans were given the traditional men's jobs, and the women with nontraditional skills were forced to compete for the traditional women's jobs with other women who had been employed in clerical and service work.

At the end of the war, the women often felt ambivalent about their veteran status, some even admitting to being ashamed of their service experience. Part of the reason is that women were often discouraged from thinking of themselves as veterans. Several government agencies claimed that they were unaware that women had become a regular part of the armed forces and thus denied them veterans' benefits in rehiring programs.[25] The Veterans of Foreign Wars took an even more active role in denying recognition to women veterans, adopting new bylaws after the war to exclude women from membership.[26]

In addition, VA hospitals were not geared to meet the needs of women veterans: Rarely did they provide any gynecological services, and many hospitals discouraged women from utilizing them because of lack of privacy.[27] The overall effect was that women were less likely than men to take advantage of their educational and medical benefits.

Thus, the majority of female veterans returned to traditional roles after the war. The question whether the women would have stayed or pursued nontraditional roles had these options been available is unanswerable. It is true, however, that the end of the war did not signal a change in women's status relative to men. While in the military, the women were in segregated, often lower-status (i.e., non-combat-rated) jobs; and because they were women, they were always considered auxiliary, temporary workers. Furthermore, the women were expected to maintain a feminine image and standards of behavior that exaggerated the qualities of morality and virtue while they were on active duty. It is therefore not surprising that so many women resumed traditional life-styles after the war.

The emotional interests behind the maintenance of gender in World War II are cast in even greater relief when we compare women in the military with another minority group, men in nursing. Men faced similar exclusionary policies in their attempts to integrate the all-female nursing corps. But what is perhaps more surprising, female military nurses often found themselves subject to the same ambivalent treatment as enlisted women, even though female nurses were in no way displacing male workers. The definition and conceptualization of femininity ensured the marginality of women in the military, regardless of the nature of their jobs.

MILITARY NURSING IN WORLD WAR II

The Army Nursing Corps was established in 1901, followed in 1908 by the Navy Nursing Corps. Few found any reason to resist the establishment of these military corps, which were composed exclusively of women. By the time World War II broke out, they were unquestionably considered an established, integral part of military operations.

Nurses responded with enthusiasm to wartime recruiting drives. The American Nurses' Association boasted that 43 percent of active RNs in the country volunteered for military service.[28] Over the course of the war, over 64,000 women joined the two nursing corps. However, the supply of nurses was never considered sufficient to meet the demands of a country at war, and both civilian and military hospitals had trouble meeting their staffing needs. Because relatively high-paying industry jobs were opening up to women, many RNs and practical nurses left the profession in search of more rewarding work. Legislation to draft nurses into the Army and Navy Nursing Corps enjoyed widespread popular support: A Gallup poll taken in February 1945 indicated that 73 percent of Americans approved of a draft of female nurses.[29] This legislation surely would have been approved had the end of the war not preempted its passage. In the interim, emotional appeals to return to their profession went out to all nurses who had quit practicing—to all young, white, female nurses, that is.

The services preferred white female nurses who were single and under forty years old.[30] The corps' inability to recruit enough suitable candidates inspired the formation of the Cadet Nursing Corps (CNC), a federally sponsored nurse training program. In its six-year history the CNC allocated $161 million to hospital schools around the country to train 125,000 nurses. Cadet nursing students were high school graduates between the ages of seventeen and twenty-five. In addition to receiving free tuition, fees, and books courtesy of the government, the cadets were paid a stipend during their study. They were not required to join the military upon graduation, however. They had only to promise to engage in "military or other Federal governmental or essential civilian services for the duration of the present war."[31]

Nurses in the army and navy were officers—but with "relative rank," meaning they were given officers' title and uniform but denied a commission, retirement benefits, dependents' allowance, and comparable pay. For example, a navy ensign nurse made $90 per month; a male ensign was paid $150 per month. Not until June 1944 did Congress pass a law granting members of the ANC and NNC true officers' rank, and even then it was "temporary rank," extending only for the duration of the war plus six months.

As with other women in the services, pregnant nurses were immediately discharged. Married women, with or without children, were not allowed to serve overseas. RNs up to the age of forty-five were accepted into the corps, although recruits tended to be much younger (the median age for army nurses was twenty-eight and a half years).[32] The possibility of extending the age limit to sixty or sixty-five was introduced in the House floor debate on the proposed legislation to draft nurses. This provision, recommended by nursing organizations, could well have been amended into the bill had the legislation ever been put up for a vote. As one House member said: "I have a notion that a great many boys when they are well would prefer a pretty blond, but when they are sick or wounded will be happy to have as a nurse a motherly woman maybe of 35 or even 45."[33] (He was under the mistaken impression that the age limit at the time was much younger.)

Military nurses did not tend soldiers directly on the field of combat. There was a complex hierarchy established wherein the nurses trained male hospital corpsmen (army) and pharmacists' mates (navy) to administer first aid on the battlefield and then transfer the wounded to hospitals behind the lines, where the nurses would tend them. In the army the corpsmen outnumbered the nurses eight to one; thus, nurses' administrative and teaching tasks took up much of their time. There were cases, however, of female nurses caught in combat and forced to work under fire.[34]

Women in the nursing corps often found themselves in the same "compromising" positions as the women in the reserves regarding their perceived role as "morale builders" for the troops. In 1946, the sociologist Edward Bernays studied wartime nursing to determine veterans' attitudes toward the nurses who served in the nursing corps. In his report he wrote,

> As to the chief contribution of nurses to victory, there were divided opinions—roughly 50-50 between professional skills and morale building. As morale builders, nurses were praised by the army sergeant . . . who said, "The infantry realizes that the nurses are immediately behind them with all their experience, to do everything for the men if they are hurt"; while another sergeant thought "the therapeutic pretty face idea is overrated." Naturally, there are two sides to the sergeant's comment, as indicated by the nurse veteran who said, "It is hard to convince the average male officer that our main duty lies with the sick, not the well."[35]

This morale-building function was considered a legitimate role of the military nurse. A popular war correspondent, Ernie Pyle, described this feature of the army nurse's role:

> One nurse was always on duty in each tentful of 20 men. . . . Most of the time the nurses wore army coveralls, but [the commanding officer] wanted them to put on dresses once in a while, for he said the effect on the men was astounding. The touch of femininity, the knowledge that a woman was around, gave the wounded man courage and confidence and a feeling of security. And the more feminine, the better.[36]

The appeals to femininity to describe and justify the nurses' contributions to the war effort sometimes shaded into slanderous accusations. Campbell notes that widespread rumors of nurses' immorality—most notably stories about their "active" social lives with top brass—caused concern on the part of recruiters and magazine editors, not to mention the nurses themselves. Predictably, the source of the malicious gossip was again found to be military servicemen.[37]

In the United States during the height of the World War II nursing shortage, there were nine thousand black female RNs and over three thousand male nurses whose services were not recruited or deemed necessary. A few male and black female nurses did ultimately serve in the military, but only because of the lobbying efforts of the National Association of Colored Graduate Nurses and the men's section of the American Nurses' Association.

Until 1948, black and white nurses belonged to separate professional associations—the National Association of Colored Graduate Nurses (NACGN) and the American Nurses' Association (ANA). Although the ANA did not bar black nurses from joining at the national level, the state ANA affiliates in some parts of the country restricted membership to whites. Before 1941, all recruits into the military nursing corps were required to belong to the ANA, which excluded blacks in some areas of the country. Not until 1941 were black women allowed to become military nurses, and even then they were limited to serving in the Army Nursing Corps. The navy excluded all black women from its nursing corps throughout the war.[38]

In early 1941 the War Department announced that the ANC would accept fifty-six black nurses. The limited number was justified within the context of racial segregation: Black nurses were allowed to work only on all-black wards in hospitals with a sufficient number of blacks to warrant having a separate ward. Black female nurses were also used to tend German prisoners of war during the war, but *not* white American soldiers.

In a biography of Mabel K. Staupers, NACGN executive secretary during the war, Darlene Clark Hine describes the justification for this racial segregation: James C. Magee, the surgeon general of the U.S. Army,

> asserted that he "would not place white soldiers in the position where they would have to accept service from Negro professionals." . . . One War Department officer would later explain to Staupers that the racial segregation supported and practiced by the U.S. Army derived from the conviction that "men who are fulfilling the same obligations, suffering the same dislocation of their private lives and wearing the identical uniform should within the confines of the military establishment, have the same privileges for rest and relaxation that they enjoyed at home."[39]

The military clearly saw nurses as providing a replacement for the services women rendered in the soldiers' private households.

In early January 1945, when proposed legislation to draft nurses was publicly announced, there were 9,000 black women RNs in the United States, 330 in the army, and none in the navy. There were also 3,000 male registered nurses who were not allowed into the nursing corps at the height of the nursing shortage.[40] Male nurses were not granted deferments, and most were drafted as privates and given little or no opportunity to use their nursing skills.

What was the justification for excluding men from the nursing corps? The U.S. surgeon general provided the following rationale: "The situation concerning male nurses is not at all parallel to that of female nurses, who are appointed for a single specific type of duty for which they are peculiarly qualified by reason of their sex." He also argued: "Army nurses of either sex must accord patients all the usual care required by the duties of their profession, including a variety of intimate offices and quasi-menial services. Women of officer rank can render these duties without incongruity, while men of such rank cannot."[41] As far as the surgeon general was concerned, nursing was women's work, and the idea that men would want to perform the often menial tasks associated with it was insulting and degrading to all men.

The Navy Department cited the "morale-building" function as an additional reason for excluding men from the nursing corps: "Another service, referred to less frequently, is the morale building effect of members of the Navy Nursing Corps on the sailors. The presence of women in the hospital is recognized as a factor in improving the morale of the men who are patients."[42] Men could not be navy nurses precisely because they were not women.

Part of the problem, according to army officials, was that the nursing corps was not geared to accommodate men who were heads of household. Because nurses had to be single or widowed to join the corps, no dependency allowance was authorized for them. In addition, army nurses were required to live in military quarters; there was no provision for living off post. Both of these reasons were cited as administrative barriers to integrating men into the corps. Thus, the argument went, men couldn't join the corps even if they were admitted because the salary and living arrangements could not support and accommodate a family.

The navy did eventually open the door to male nurses—albeit the back door. Male nurses were allowed to request assignment as pharmacist's mate, second class, in the hospital corps (not the nursing corps). These men performed several nursing duties (as well as other functions), but they were not *called* nurses. They earned $2 per week more than nurses even though they were not commissioned as officers, as the nurses were. In addition, they qualified for extra housing allowances and other dependency benefits if they were married.

The men's section of the American Nurses' Association lobbied to change the military's policies on granting deferments to male nurses, allowing men to enter the Army and Navy Nursing Corps, and allowing men to train in the Cadet Nursing Corps.[43] Although these campaigns were largely unsuccessful, the arguments made on behalf of the male nurses are interesting because they reveal a concern similar to the military's in the maintenance of gender boundaries. The following is a 1944 statement by the men's section of the ANA:

> [There is a] need for realistic planning by nursing to provide representative nursing care for men patients with special provisions in urology [and psychiatry]. . . . It was urged that the objectives set up should include *careful selection* of men student nurses, assurance for the student and his advisers that nursing offers him a field in which as a graduate he will find opportunity for *leadership* and *supervision, teaching,* and other nursing activities where *well-qualified men nurses are needed.*[44]

The ANA frequently argued that male patients would be served best by male attendants, particularly in the areas of psychiatric nursing (where men's presumed greater strength would be valuable in controlling violent patients) and urology. In a letter to Congress, one male nurse wrote on the subject of psychiatric and genitourinary diseases: "In certain types of conditions, male patients have particularly appreciated our relieving the embarrassment occasioned when women performed these duties, and often the treatment has been much more effective just because the barrier of sex was removed."[45] Thus, sex differences were called upon to provide the grounds for including men in the female domain of nursing. Ironically, the army later used the same reasoning to justify men's continued *exclusion* from the corps: "Army nurses are qualified for assignment to any service in the hospital, whereas the assignment of men nurses would be restricted to men's wards."[46] According to the military, the male nurses' specialized skills would limit their duty assignments, which would conflict with basic military policy that no personnel be accepted on limited duty.

The male nurses did not dispute the military's argument that female nurses played an important morale-building function for the troops. Nor did they suggest that men could perform this service equally well. In fact the men's section of the ANA set itself the task of recruiting a "strong type of man student to enroll in accredited schools of nursing."[47] Male nurses would not fulfill the feminine role expected of the women; an entirely different emotional affect would be expected of the men. A 1945 appeal to increase the number of male students in accredited nursing schools alerted recruiters to the sort of man considered appropriate for the profession: The nursing profession needs to promote "careful screening of applicants before admission and early elimination of enrolled students who seem lacking in interest or aptitude. Particular emphasis should be placed on the importance of selecting men students who are definitely masculine."[48] The male nurses argued that aggressive, masculine men were needed to fill administrative and leadership positions within the nursing corps: "There is need of a program which will include careful selection, teaching and supervision of orderlies and attendants. Registered men nurses are needed for the leadership and teaching involved."[49] Female nurses were in charge of these functions when this was written, and no evidence or opinions of unsatisfactory job performance were cited. But promoting men to leadership and teaching roles rendered their presence within nursing less threatening to opponents of integration and more desirable by the "type of man" the ANA was seeking to recruit.

Additionally, it was believed that men would be better providers of care in dangerous environments. The following is a quote from a *Look* magazine article on female nurses:

> In a recent 6,000 miles of travel from end to end of the Pacific theater, every man I met agreed that his part of the war would go better without American women in the forward areas. Army and Navy doctors, even nurses themselves, will admit the female nurses

in forward areas do nothing male Medical Corps men cannot do better. And do without the protective worrying of those officers and men who don't like to see women shot at.[50]

CONCLUSION

The experiences of women in the military and the nursing corps in World War II illustrate that the erosion of occupational sex segregation does not necessarily challenge gender differences. Military policymakers were obsessed with preserving and maintaining gender differences, and this concern reverberated throughout both the propaganda and the slander campaigns directed at women in the services. The official and unofficial treatment of women in the military during this period reflects an ambivalence toward femininity that in part constitutes masculinity. On the one hand, women's presence in the military was justified with appeals to stereotypically feminine characteristics: Wartime propaganda urged that women's "special skills"—including their nurturant qualities, manual dexterity, and propensity for repetitious tasks—were desperately needed for fighting and winning the war. On the other hand, stereotypes of femininity were at the root of the slanderous rumors and special restrictions that detracted from women's contributions to the war effort. Women were circumscribed by fearful beliefs about their sexuality: They were alternately accused of being lesbians or prostitutes and subject to numerous regulations regarding marriage, pregnancy, and their moral standards. This madonna/whore imagery of womanhood has deep roots in masculine psychology, and because the military has been overwhelmingly male-dominated, this very imagery has framed women's treatment in it.

We have seen how the importance of gender to military policymakers also barred men who wanted to enter an all-female preserve. Maintaining femininity was literally given priority over acquiring personnel to nurse wounded soldiers, despite the widespread perception of a national nursing shortage. Yet even those men who sought to enter nursing couched their demands in terms of gender. Men would be better nurses because of attributes women lacked. They argued that if men were allowed to nurse, soldiers and officers would no longer have to worry about vulnerable women at the front lines, male soldiers would no longer be subject to embarrassing scenarios in the hospital room, and the leadership and instruction of hospital corpsmen would improve.

All these concerns voiced by the male nurses appeal *not* to the capabilities of women in the military service, but rather to service *men's* inability to accept women's participation in the war effort. No one ever questioned the performance of women in the field: The nurses at Bataan and Corregidor, for example, received full military recognition and honors for their performance in combat. The issue then was the same one that limited women's role in the reserves: To men in the services, women posed a threat *not* to their jobs, but to something much deeper:

> A woman's army to defend the United States of America. Think of the humiliation. What has become of the manhood of America, that we have to call on our women to do what has ever been the duty of men? The thing is so revolting to me, to my sense of Americanism, to my sense of decency that I just cannot discuss it in a vein that I think legislation should be discussed on the floor of this House.[51]

The men's masculinity—their own gender identity—was threatened by the presence of women, a psychological and largely unconscious threat reflected in the ideology of femininity enforced on military women.

Because the military was so closely associated with masculinity, the presence of women was particularly threatening to men. If women could perform tasks that previously only "masculine" men could supposedly do, the activity itself was devalued in men's eyes because the masculine goal of separation from feminine identification is challenged. Because women were needed in the war effort, it was essential to military men ideologically to circumscribe women's roles in the military—to define their roles in such a way so as not to challenge the masculinity of men engaged in identical tasks. Only by distinguishing men's and women's contributions could soldiering remain attractive to the sort of "masculine" men policymakers had always sought to recruit.

The ideology of femininity in World War II reflects military men's irrational interest in preserving the masculinity of the military. The social organization of the military—its overwhelming male dominance—is what gave men the power to enforce their definitions of femininity on female soldiers. It is one thing to desire to separate and distinguish oneself from women and another to enforce that separation on others.

The women who served during World War II did not perceive any incongruity between their military work and their gender identity. Why shouldn't women work on airplanes, track radar, or pack parachutes? These activities did not threaten their femininity; the veterans I spoke with did not feel compelled to recast their contributions to the war effort in "feminine" terms (in contrast to the male nurses). However, they did feel defensive about the slanderous accusations made by their male counterparts. The women submitted to restrictions on their behavior during World War II as a means to counter the suggestive rumors about them. They realized that by stepping outside the restrictions official policy imposed on them, they were opening themselves up to abuse from male soldiers.

New recruits today still encounter the problems faced by the women who entered the military during World War II. I now turn to the contemporary status of women in the military.

3

Femininity in the Marine Corps

There is no question but that women could do a lot of things in the military services. So could men in wheelchairs. But you couldn't expect the services to want a whole company of people in wheelchairs.

General Lewis Hershey,
former Selective Service Director[1]

American women have fought a long, uphill battle to be allowed to join the military during peacetime, and only recently have their efforts met with any success. Women now make up approximately 10 percent of the United States military—a 500 percent increase in the number of women on active duty since 1972. The United States has a greater component of women in the military than any other modern Western military. Today women are employed in practically every job specialty—except those that would involve them directly in combat—and they work alongside men throughout the army, navy, air force, and marines.

The percentage of women in the different branches ranges from 4.57 percent in the marines to 11.12 percent in the air force. The reasons for this range has to do with what is called the "teeth-to-tail" ratio (the number of actual combat fighters to the number of troops required for administrative and technical support). The air force, the most "technological" of the services, requires the most ground support personnel to maintain each fighter; it therefore has the most women. A greater proportion of Marine Corps troops is involved in direct fighting—it has a low "teeth-to-tail" ratio; therefore, fewer women are found in this branch.

Each service sets its own recruiting standards and limits on the accessions of female recruits. Even though all men and women enlisting in the military take the same entrance examination, the branches have different minimum acceptable scores. Potential recruits are grouped in categories labeled I–V. People in categories I–III are actively recruited, and people scoring in category V (known as mental deficients) are not allowed to join the military. Men in category IV are permitted to join in limited numbers; women in this group are excluded outright.

The army and the marines have more discrepant entrance standards for men and women than the other branches. Both accept men who are high school dropouts; in fact, the Marine Corps accepts male applicants who have completed only the tenth grade and may waive even that standard in the case of "exceptionally" qualified applicants.[2] But all female applicants must have a high school diploma; they do not accept the G.E.D. as an equivalent.

The different entrance standards for male and female recruits is but one of several official policies that discriminate against women and institutionalize gender differences in the military. Perhaps the most detrimental of these policies are the combat exclusionary rules, which prohibit women from firing line-of-sight weapons. These rules bar women from the most prestigious military specialties, for firing weapons is, after all, the raison d'être of the military, and combat is the most highly rewarded activity in terms of honor and promotion.

Not surprisingly, women's advocacy groups are today clamoring to repeal these restrictive policies, thus putting political pressure on policymakers to justify the exclusion of women. These policymakers commission study after study to document the elusive differences between men and women, exploring everything from women's upper body strength, to their morale in integrated combat units, to their femininity in order to justify excluding them from combat specialties. An air force captain who was a subject in a study evaluating women in pilot training school said this of her instruction: "It was a test program; they wanted to monitor how the women were doing. . . . The first classes had it bad, with a lot of bad feelings between the men and the women because the women

were treated special. Everything they did was monitored by head-
quarters. It was almost like they were treated different so they had
to act different." This "search for difference" belies the military's
fundamental unwillingness to accept women into its ranks. As I will
show, not one of these studies has found that women as a group are
either incapable or "substandard" compared to men as a group. Yet
the discriminatory policies remain.

In this chapter I explore the reasons for the military's unwillingness to accept women. To some extent these policies can be interpreted as military men's efforts to maintain their monopolies of
power and status. Excluding women from prestigious specialties
limits the competition for the available jobs. However, this unwillingness emanates in large part from issues directly related to gender. Women are discriminated against in the military because of
its close association with masculinity.

Our society defines masculinity in contradistinction to femininity; a masculine person is one who denies and to some extent
denigrates qualities associated with femininity. Think, for example, of the expressions young boys use to criticize their fellows for
not living up to the standards of their newfound masculine status:
"Sissy," "crybaby," "momma's boy" all describe derogatory attitudes toward the affective and nurturant characteristics closely
associated with femininity. The military is an institutionalized
version of this "masculine" position. Policymakers define the military as an arena limited to tough men able to "make the grade";
basic training is intentionally marketed as a "masculinity proving
ground." A recent advertisement for the Army National Guard,
showing a group of men wading through thigh-high water, is
captioned "kiss your momma goodbye." This close association of
the military with masculinity actually precludes the equal treatment of men and women, as demonstrated by the justifications for
discriminatory treatment of women.

Consider the example of umbrella use. Army and Marine Corps
men are not allowed to use umbrellas while in uniform, although
women in all the services are. Why the difference? According to a

thirdhand newspaper account, umbrella use by men was vetoed because senior officers thought the practice "too wimpy."[3] Officials' desires to maintain the masculinity of the military reverberate throughout every level of policy and practice—with serious (as well as trivial) consequences for how military women are treated and considered.

But an understanding of official policy is only part of the story. The women who are subject to these regulations have their own stories to tell. In the second part of this chapter, military women describe their on-the-job experiences, indicating how policies directly influence their daily work lives. At the end of this chapter, I discuss these women's opinions of the policies and how they see their place within the military.

OFFICIAL POLICY

The 1970s witnessed dramatic changes in the accession and deployment of women in the military. At the start of the all-volunteer force a few years after the end of the Vietnam War, growing concern about recruiting shortfalls led the Defense Department to recommend utilizing more women to fill the military's depleting ranks. A 1977 report claimed that enlisting more women would improve the overall quality of recruits and save the Defense Department over $1 billion per year. Women would improve the quality of recruits because they are, on average, better educated than men (they are more likely to be high school graduates). And recruiting more women would save money because lucrative bonus plans were not needed to fill the military's female quotas with "high-quality" recruits (i.e., high school graduates). (This suggests that women may have more limited civilian employment opportunities than men.) The report concludes:

> The tradeoff in today's recruiting market is between a high quality female and a low quality male. The average woman available to be recruited is smaller, weighs less, and is physically weaker than the vast majority of male recruits. She is also much brighter,

better educated (a high school graduate), scores much higher on the aptitude tests and is much less likely to become a disciplinary problem.[4]

This report represents a radical shift in Defense Department policy toward women, which has traditionally opposed their participation in the military. It downplays any differences between men and women and urges the various branches to reassess and revise their combat exclusionary policies.

But policymakers in all branches of the services did not share the report's conclusions. For example, although the study projects that the number of women in the army could double by 1983, the army argued that the current number of women ought to be frozen:[5] "We should err on the side of national security until such time as we have confidence that the basic mission of the army can be accomplished with significantly more female content in the active force."[6]

The army then conducted a series of studies designed to test the impact of women on combat support field units. One of these tests, MAXWAC, was designed to assess the effects of varying percentages of women soldiers assigned to different types of combat support units. The "woman content" was controlled at two intervals in this experiment: In some units the percentage varied from 0 percent to 15 percent; in others it varied from 15 percent to the maximum, 35 percent. (The army presumed that negative effects of increasing "woman content" would be perceived somewhere between 0 percent and 35 percent.) The study found "that the number of women (up to as much as 35%) had no significant effect on the operational capability of specific Category II and III company size units."[7] In addition, the researchers (from the Army Research Institute) note, the enlisted women "observed in the units were motivated and doing an excellent job. EW accomplished physically demanding tasks by utilizing leverage and a peer helper when required. EW appeared to do better in units where they were treated as equals and the leadership was supportive."[8]

Unconvinced, the army commissioned additional studies, one entitled REFWAC that carefully studied women during sustained combat exercises in Europe. Again, no adverse impact on unit performance was discovered.

Thus, unable to document any harmful effects of increasing the number of women in uniform, in 1978 Secretary of Defense Harold Brown ordered the number of enlisted women to be doubled by 1983. That brought the total number of enlisted women allowed to approximately 330,000, over 10 percent of the total forces.

If the army had shown that up to 35 percent of its combat support troops could be female with no adverse consequences, why was the projection of female accessions limited to 10 percent? Recruitment goals seem lower still when compared to 1976 Brookings Institution projections. A study conducted there estimated that one-third of *all* military jobs could be filled by women—including 76.1 percent of all jobs in the air force.[9]

Military combat exclusionary policies are the main obstacles to recruiting more women. These policies are part of Title 10 of the U.S. Code: Section 6015 prohibits women from working on navy combat vessels; Section 8549 prohibits women from operating fighter jets in the air force. Ironically, the army is not *legally* restricted from deploying women in combat zones, but internal policy prohibits them from serving where there is a high probability of combat occurring.

Relatively few specialties are closed to women as a result of the combat exclusionary rules—a fact that the Department of Defense frequently advertises. However, a high proportion of *positions* are closed to women. Table 1 describes this discrepancy. The figures are somewhat misleading insofar as they suggest that women could potentially make up 90 percent of the air force or 20 percent of the marines. Issues other than specialty skill are involved. A certain proportion of positions are designated for men only to ensure proper "rotation" from overseas combat tours back to the United States. Women are also restricted from serving where sex

Table 1. Skills and Positions Open to Women in the Military

	Army (%)	Navy (%)	Air Force (%)	Marines (%)
Skills	90	79	98	80
Positions	53	49	90	20

Source: U.S. Department of Defense, Manpower Installations and Logistics, *Military Women in the Department of Defense*, 1984, p. v.

segregated living facilities are not available—usually a problem overseas.

Another limitation is the Marine Corps' insistence that women cannot make up more than 10 percent of any unit. The reasoning behind this is that if a unit were called to deploy—a situation the Marine Corps claims would require the removal of all female personnel—the unit would still have 90 percent of its strength, sufficient to accomplish its mission.[10]

One final limitation on women entering the service involves career progression. Several military career paths require combat command experience. Because women are restricted from combat, the service branches must devise alternative paths to make it possible for them to advance in rank. These paths are limited in number because the military rewards its combat veterans with the highest honors and the highest rank. Thus, the number of positions effectively open to women is restricted.

One consequence of these exclusionary policies is that women are overrepresented in noncombat occupational specialties. They make up 12.4 percent of all communications and intelligence specialists, 11.8 percent of all medical and dental personnel, and 36.6 percent of administration and functional support personnel. This latter category includes the subspecialties of personnel, clerical, and data processing. Thus, the majority of women in uniform are employed in "traditional" occupations (see Table 2).

Another consequence of these policies is that women tend to be concentrated in the lower ranks. There are approximately 20 percent more women than men in the four lowest pay grades, and

Table 2.   Percent Female in Enlisted Occupational Specialties

	Department of Defense	Army	Navy	Air Force	Marines
Infantry	0.4	1.0	1.0	0.3	0.0
Elec. Equip. Repair	4.8	2.7	5.4	7.4	3.7
Communications and Intelligence	12.4	13.4	13.4	10.0	7.7
Medical and Dental	11.8	14.1	13.1	10.4	0.0[a]
Technical Specialist	2.5	2.7	2.0	2.7	2.3
Administration and Functional Support	36.6	39.5	28.1	37.8	35.5
Elec./Mech. Repair	7.6	6.0	6.4	10.4	5.0
Crafts	1.7	0.7	1.3	2.7	1.7
Service and Supply	9.5	10.7	5.0	10.7	11.7

Source: U.S. Department of Defense, Manpower Installations and Logistics, *Military Women in the Department of Defense,* 1984, pp. 45–47.

[a]The Marine Corps does not have a separate hospital corps.

men outnumber women in the four highest pay grades eight to one.[11] The Defense Department argues that this is because military women have accrued fewer years of service than men (on average). Data do suggest that women who reenlist are promoted slightly faster than men. Yet these studies fail to examine why women have a higher attrition rate; their exclusion from specific specialties could contribute to their decision to resign.

A debate has raged for years on whether women belong in combat. The most frequent argument made by opponents of women in combat is that women's lesser physical capacities mandate their exclusion from frontline combat: "If two ground combat forces meet in battle and one is composed, in part, of physically inferior personnel, the other has a distinct tactical advantage. The physically weaker unit will be defeated. Equal opportunity on the battlefield spells defeat."[12] Opponents also argue that public sentiment runs against so using women in the military. They argue that the defeat of the equal rights amendment was in part a response to public dismay that women would be drafted alongside men.[13]

Another argument that opponents of women in combat often make is that women in foxholes would damage the camaraderie of the male troops. An army major warns that the "psychological ties of male bonding in the warrior group may be eroded by the presence of women."[14] Furthermore, there must be a "girl back home" who the soldier is fighting to protect. Mixing the sexes in combat might destroy that essential motivation.

Many are opposed to integrating combat because they fear the development of sexual relationships that would distract the troops from fighting the enemy. One of the major obstacles to integrating the Titan missile silos, for example, was official concern that the intimate contact involved in this duty would interfere with accomplishing the job (the silos are staffed by two crew members who work together in very close quarters). The compromise reached mandates that crews be composed of same-sex members. On the issue of women sharing foxholes with men, no compromise has yet been suggested.

Advocates for women in combat downplay the importance of the physical strength differences between men and women. In the navy and the air force, the strength differences do not pose a problem: The physical strength required to fly a fighter plane or serve on a combat navy vessel is within the capacity of most women. For this reason, the air force women I interviewed were the most vehement in their opposition to the combat restrictions. An instructor pilot complained, "Over 75 percent of the aircraft we have in the air force we [female pilots] can't fly. . . . I'm fighter-qualified—that's why I'm an instructor, and I can't fly a fighter!"

Some argue that many women could also do well in the sort of direct fighting engaged in by army and marine soldiers. Pointing out that physical strength varies greatly among individuals—even among men—they argue that sex should not be the sole criterion for determining who is fit and who is unfit to serve in combat. A standardized strength test should be used instead.

Advocates for women in combat often criticize the tenuous distinctions between jobs that are open and closed to women. Women are assigned to Titan missile silos, for example, but they are prohibited from becoming fighter pilots or embassy security guards. Mady Segal points out that women are not excluded from positions in which they might be killed; women are stationed within miles of the Soviet border. Rather, women are excluded from specialities in which they might be called upon to do the killing in a direct, premeditated fashion.[15] Women are prevented from entering army jobs that would routinely engage them in direct combat but not from positions that could occasionally expose them to combat. She also notes that air force women are allowed to fly tankers into and around combat zones, but are prohibited from flying fighter planes in the same area.[16] Judith Stiehm likens these policies to a "male protection racket": Women, she notes, are supposed to be "protected" by a group of men, which prohibits women from taking up arms themselves.[17]

The combat exclusionary policies are not entirely immune to official dissent. In 1979 the Department of Defense proposed House legislation to eliminate Sections 6015 and 8547 of Title 10, the air force and navy policies restricting women from combat. The Department of Defense wrote to Congress:

> The term "combat" refers to "engaging an enemy or being engaged by an enemy in armed conflict." . . . Women have served in combat in many skills during World War II, Korea, and Vietnam. Army nurses have served in combat for over a hundred years, although they and other medical personnel are considered noncombatants. Since the word "combat" has historically been used to include such a broad range of activities, the Department of Defense does not believe that the term provides a useful basis for expanding the opportunities for women in the service.[18]

The Department of Defense opposed the combat restrictions because they severely limit the number of women accepted into the military. Their efforts to repeal these policies are understand-able because they were made when women were being consid-ered as a potential resource to augment the dwindling pool of military recruits.

This effort was also motivated by the recognition of the logisti-cal problems that would arise should women not be allowed in combat when war breaks out. The idea that all women would be immediately removed from their integrated duty stations and shipped home in the event of a war seemed ludicrous to some, especially because the military had invested so much time and train-ing in its increasingly specialized troops—both male and female.[19]

However, in spite of these arguments at the time of the congres-sional hearings, support for repeal of the combat restrictions was by no means unanimous. General William Westmoreland com-mented during House hearings: "The political administration is trying to use the military as a vehicle to further social change in our society . . . in utter disregard for potential fighting effective-ness. . . . No man with gumption wants a woman to fight his battles."[20]

Opponents of the repeal won the day in Congress. In fact, Department of Defense policy toward women underwent a radi-cal shift soon after these efforts to repeal the combat restrictions were defeated. In 1980, Ronald Reagan was elected president, and almost overnight the Defense Department's aggressive efforts to sexually integrate the military were halted. One month after Rea-gan took office, the army limit on female accessions was capped at 65,000, the number of women on active duty at the time. Officials reported that this action was prompted by military commanders' concern that the women's ranks had grown too fast: Apparently, all the army's commanders had recommended *reducing* the num-ber of enlisted women to between 52,000 and 55,000.[21] However, no data were cited to confirm the harmful effects of women in the military. In fact, General Robert G. Yerks, a chief of the army personnel staff involved with the change in policy, acknowledged, "It was not that women were not doing their jobs. . . . Most are

doing a really fine job . . . they are valuable and productive soldiers."[22] Assistant Defense Secretary Lawrence Korb granted temporary approval to the caps on female accession as requested by
the military commanders, pending the results of yet another study
on women in the army.

Representative Patricia Schroeder (D-Colorado), member of
the House Armed Services Committee, vehemently opposed the
new limits, pointing out, "The implication there is [that former
President] Carter never made any studies. Women have been studied all along. Women get the sense that 'they don't want us
here.' "[23] Senator William Proxmire (D-Wisconsin) charged that
the army was "just using the new administration as an excuse to
deny women equal pay, promotion and enlistment rights."[24]

But the halt on female accessions was not directly motivated by
a desire to dismantle equal opportunity policies for women in the
military. The economy was in a recession, and the high unemploy-
ment rate was enabling the services to meet their enlistment quotas without resorting to women.[25] This factor—combined with
Reagan's increased defense spending, which raised military personnel's wages and benefits—was making the military an attractive
option to young men again. To the field commanders' way of
thinking, there was no reason to accept female soldiers when men
were available to do the job, no matter how competent the
women were. Apparently, this had been their thinking all along,
but it took the new political and economic climate to produce
policy changes that reflected their prejudices.[26]

Soon after capping female accessions, in May 1982, the army
ended a four-year "experiment" (as it was then called) with integrated basic training. For three years, male and female recruits had
been brought together for practically all aspects of training, including rifle marksmanship, first aid, and physical training. The army
decided to halt this practice reportedly because "it feels the men
are not being challenged enough."[27] Captain Douglas Haywood
of the Army Training Command explained on a radio talk show,
"The reason we did this was that we found, through observation

basically, that men were not fully physically challenged when they went through basic training with women. . . . This in no way reflects upon [women's] ability to be good soldiers. And they are good soldiers and serve competently throughout the army."[28]

Sharon Lord, the defense secretary for equal opportunity, who opposed this change, lamented, "No one provided any data that showed integrated training was not successful. I was alarmed that the Army would make a major change without data. The Army should have provided that."[29]

The decision to resegregate basic training came before the results of the latest study on women in the army were released. This study, called WITA (for Women in the Army), was shrouded in secrecy, and its publication was delayed several times, causing anxiety among many women in uniform.[30] When it was finally released, in August 1982, its conclusions confirmed that those fears were warranted. WITA recommended the closing of twenty-three additional occupational specialties to women, bringing the total number of off-limit military occupational specialties (MOSs) to sixty-one.

The army study group based its recommendation on a complicated "direct combat probability code" that rated each army specialty on an ordinal scale ranging from "least likely to encounter direct combat" to "most likely to engage routinely in combat." This scale was designed specifically to get women out of potential combat areas.[31]

The WITA study group recognized the enormous difficulty its recommendations presented because the concept of a "combat zone" makes very little sense today given modern warfare techniques. So they had to define what direct combat *is* in order to justify excluding women from it. Here is the definition they developed:

> Direct combat is engaging an enemy with individual or crew-served weapons while being exposed to direct enemy fire, a high probability of direct physical contact with the enemy's personnel, and a substantial risk of capture. Direct combat takes place while

closing with the enemy by fire, maneuver, or shock effect in order
to destroy or capture him, or while repelling his assault by fire,
close combat or counterattack.[32]

The closure of these additional jobs resulted in an overall closure
of 76 percent of all army positions. Among the jobs now closed to
women were diver, construction surveyor, and interior electrician.
Four additional areas, mainly in chemical fields, were also at risk
of being closed to women, according to General Ronald Zeltman,
director of the WITA study group, because "they might pose a
health hazard to women of child-bearing age."[33]

Particularly upsetting to the opponents of these measures is
the fact that the army is *not* legally required to restrict women
from combat. Because there is no law prohibiting women from
serving in any occupation, army officials were rather hard-
pressed to justify their new restrictions. Defense Secretary Korb
argued that in closing more job categories to women, "the administration was merely reflecting the mood of Congress and the
public by keeping women out of combat related jobs."[34] Field
commanders' dissatisfaction with women's job performance was
also cited as a reason for the cutbacks: "Army field officers [have
increasingly complained] about what they called women's poor
performance in some jobs and . . . high turnover in some units,
caused by women dropping out of the Army because of unhappi-
ness in their jobs. . . . The women's drop-out rate is 14% ahead
of the rate for men, [Defense Secretary] Korb said."[35] What the
Department of Defense did *not* publicize were the reasons wom-
en's attrition rates were so high. Congress earlier had ascribed
this high dropout rate to sexual harassment and "males' inability
to accept women in untraditional jobs." It ordered the army to
remedy this discrepancy.[36]

There is some evidence that women in nontraditional specialties are more harassed than those in traditional specialties, such as
the clerical fields, but few women escape this type of treatment
altogether. According to a study of first-term female marines,

Forty two percent reported being excluded from something on the basis of sex; 14 percent, being refused field experience; 39 percent, being discriminated against; and 36 percent, being treated with favoritism. . . . When the women were asked to state the worst thing about being a woman Marine, 53 percent cited harassment and another 39 percent, differential treatment.[37]

Those critical of the high attrition rates of women in nontraditional specialties seldom mention the scope of this problem. Instead, they blame women for their failure to adapt to these new environments:

While it is unknown whether the frequency of colorful or obscene language is increasing in the Army, Woelfel and Savell show that women's job satisfaction is negatively related to the frequency of vulgar and obscene language they perceive to be directed at them. . . . The sample size is small, but indicative of another area of Army life *where women might experience adjustment problems.*[38]

The "adjustment problems" women face in these nontraditional fields are used to justify barring women from them altogether.

The complicated story of the combat exclusionary policies reveals the sensitivity of official policy toward women in the military to political and economic pressures. In recent years there has been a backlash against women's infiltration into this formerly all-male preserve. Although this can be seen in part as a reflection of the conservative agenda of the Reagan administration, the military has never welcomed women into the regular ranks with open arms. Without the mounting economic pressure to increase women's role in the armed forces, military officials would probably not have permitted the women's ranks to grow at such astounding rates during the mid 1970s. Even so, the numerous studies of women in the military during this period can be seen as attempts to resist their incursion: Each sought to discover ways that women compare unfavorably with men in order to justify excluding them from military service. Despite findings of no or little differentiation, once there was political support to justify excluding women again, the cutbacks began.

None of the studies undertaken ever revealed any crucial differences between male and female soldiers' abilities to perform their duties. The main justification for limiting women's participation in the armed services was the perception on the part of line officers and commanders that women were not measuring up—this in spite of the fact that such officials rarely came into contact with enlisted women in the field or recruits going through basic training.

In essence, the justification for increasing women's military participation during the mid 1970s was the same as that used during World War II: to make up recruiting shortfalls—a perceived emergency. Once that emergency subsided, women were once again excluded from this traditionally masculine occupation.

Official means in addition to the combat restriction policies are also used to limit and circumscribe women's role in the military. Segregation of men and women in basic training is one of these. The Marine Corps has integrated officer training but has always segregated enlisted recruit training. It is not unusual for military women to feel as though they've been "thrown to the wolves" when, after completing training, they arrive at their first duty station: Their experience in basic training does not prepare them for a work environment in which they may be the only female.

No legal provisions in any of the service branches justify segregated training, and none of the numerous studies on women in the military revealed any reasons to continue segregation. In fact, both men and women seem to perform as well, if not better, in integrated environments. One Woman Marine recruit who had previously completed integrated army basic training explained why she preferred training alongside men: "With the men you always had motivation. You're doing the three-mile run, and there's a man in front of you, and you think, 'I can catch him.' It makes you feel good to think you can compete with them on the same level." A report published during the period of integrated training noted that the presence of women did not lower morale, but in many cases tended to raise it. The report stated, "There was very little evidence of disfunctional male-versus-female competition."[39]

The key to understanding the segregation of training is military officials' belief that women "soften" basic training. The Marine Corps "asserts that the physical standards of male recruit training are necessarily rigorous and that it cannot adjust, *or appear to adjust,* this training to adapt to women's capabilities, because that would undercut the basic training concept."[40] Regardless of whether training standards are compromised in fact, the sight of women mastering the feats of basic training makes it appear that the training is not rigorous enough. Some officials even fear that if women were integrated with men in basic training, men would no longer enlist. One army major argued, "A turning away from military service because it has become something a 'girl can do' may seriously affect the Army's ability to recruit sufficient manpower."[41] If women succeed at training, the response is not to accept them as equals in the Marine Corps, but rather to conclude that there's something wrong—or soft—with the training.

Until October 1985, Women Marine recruit basic training took eight and one-half weeks, compared to twelve weeks for the men. Women were not trained to use any weaponry. Although they were all issued the M-16 rifle, they were allowed to fire it only on one day of training (after which they would spend weeks cleaning it for inspection). As of October, the women's training was extended to ten weeks, and now they are required to qualify with the rifle and to learn fighting maneuvers and how to handle mines and grenades. These changes are all considered *defensive* measures: In the order outlining the new policy, Marine Corps Commandant Paul Kelley wrote that the women "must be trained in defensive techniques and operations in the event of unforeseen hostile activity."[42] These changes in training do not imply that women will soon be entering closed combat specialties; unless Women Marines enter the military police occupational specialty, they are still prohibited from using these weapons skills once they leave training.

Male and female marines are completely separated throughout

training. The only time they see each other is during religious services on Sundays, and then they are prohibited from talking—or even looking—at each other. One recruit described this aspect of basic training to me: "We can't even look at guys. If we smile, they [the drill instructors] kill us. Keep your eyeballs straight ahead. You can't look; you can't wink. Even if you look like you're thinking about doing it, you're in trouble." One result is that men and women know very little about each other's training regimens. What they do know they learn from the Marine Corps Handbook, a basic training manual issued to all new recruits intended to enable "an enlisted man to sustain himself on the battlefield and [enable] an enlisted man or woman to function effectively in garrison and to practice those personal and professional traits characteristic of Marines."[43] Throughout the text, photos and drawings of male marines are used to illustrate various procedures and maneuvers.

The only two places female marines receive any mention are in the chapter on physical fitness (which details the different weight and strength requirements for men and women) and the chapter on clothing and grooming regulations. In the section on grooming regulations, the manual discusses appropriate standards for the two sexes. Men's "hair shall be worn neatly and closely trimmed. It may be clipped at the edges of the side and back and will be evenly graduated from zero length at the hairline on the lower portion of the head up to a maximum of 3 inches on the top of the head." Women's "hair shall be neatly shaped and arranged in an attractive, feminine style. . . . Hair may touch the collar but may not fall below the collar's lower edge. . . . If dyes, tints, or bleaches are used on the hair, the artificial color must harmonize with the person's complexion tone and eye color."[44] The very language used to describe women's regulations—"attractive," "feminine," "harmonize"—suggests less vigorous standards than those enforced on men.

Cutting off hair is a traditional rite of basic training. Marine Corps recruiters emphasize that women do *not* have to cut their hair. Regulations state that they are allowed to pin it up as long as it does not fall below the collar and the pins are inconspicuous. However, most new women recruits are pressured to cut their hair despite these rules: Because they have only ten minutes to shower and groom themselves in the morning, most are unable to meet the specifications for keeping long hair. Thus, women also have to go through this traumatic rite of passage, much to their collective dismay. But because this fact is not advertised, the impression is maintained that women's recruit training is less exacting and less traumatic than men's.

The section on hair regulations in the Marine Corps basic training manual is followed by rules governing makeup application. All Women Marine recruits are *required* to wear makeup; the minimum acceptable amount is eyeshadow and lipstick. They take classes on makeup, hair care, poise, and etiquette.[45]

The Marine Corps is especially concerned about maintaining the femininity of its female recruits—it is the only branch with the makeup requirement. A previous base commander at Parris Island, home of Women Marine recruit training, commissioned several studies on the "defeminization" of Women Marines. This is how one staff sergeant described her participation to me:

> I was told that he [a Marine Corps captain] was going to ask us questions on, more or less, the defeminization of women in recruit training. . . . We went in to this big conference room, and he asked us questions like "Did drill instructor school make you change your voice in any way to sound more masculine?" . . . I guess because they're worried about us sounding like men. . . . He asked us questions like "Did we feel any less feminine when we were on the drill field?" All the questions revolved around femininity, or us being feminine.

The same commander who commissioned the femininity tests issued orders prohibiting women from riding motorcycles on post and from wearing blue jeans while they were off duty on the island. While on duty, women drill instructors are not allowed to wear the slacks version of their uniforms; they are ordered to wear the skirt version (unless it is 32 degrees or lower).

On the surface it does seem ironic that the branch of the military most closely associated with masculinity seems most concerned with preserving women's femininity. Judith Stiehm offers one possible explanation for this phenomenon, arguing that officials' concern that military women may lose their femininity actually reflects men's insecurity about their own gender identity. In her study of the integration of the U.S. Air Force Academy, she notes that men's masculinity seemed to be threatened when women entered this previously all-male environment. For example, she tells the story of a woman officer who was given two Christmas tree balls from her superior officer, implying that she had "castrated" him.[46]

Military men's opposition to sexual integration cannot be explained entirely by the economic interests at stake in reserving all the best military jobs for themselves. This imagery of castrating females, for example, strongly suggests some deeper, underlying motive for men's refusal to accept women. The strident concerns so many military men expressed about the consequences of integration hint at the existence of some irrational forces in operation: "An aspect bearing directly upon the ability of military groups to integrate females is that it is likely to require among the male members their complete redefinition of themselves as 'men.' "[47]

The irony of this threat that women pose to the masculinity of ostensibly "macho" marines dissipates when we use psychoanalytic theory to explore the nature of masculinity. Psychoanalysis is uniquely able to supply us with insight into the unconscious and often irrational interests served by certain socially institutionalized practices. In the case of the military, it provides us with a way of understanding what is at stake in preserving masculinity by tracing the psychological conflicts that characterize it to their origins in early childhood experiences. According to psychoanalysts, the very process of achieving a masculine gender identity entails an unconscious rejection and denigration of femininity—precisely as we have observed it in the military.

The starting point for understanding the etiology of gender

identity—and therefore the reasons femininity so threatens masculinity—is the family. The organization of child rearing is crucial for determining how people experience gender later in life. The apparently mundane fact that women in our society are the primary caretakers of infants is actually the key to understanding why men are threatened by women in adult life. As Lillian Rubin points out, "no fact of our early life has greater consequences for how girls and boys develop into women and men, [and] therefore for how we relate to each other in our adult years."[48]

Psychoanalysts argue that all children who are primarily cared for by women start off life with an original feminine identification. The mother is the "original" fulfiller of all our desires and hence the object of our most intense affectionate longing. Psychoanalysts believe that the child "internalizes" the mother (i.e., assumes those characteristics associated with her). Because the mother is female, and qualities associated with her are defined as feminine, the child becomes "feminine-identified."

This original feminine-identification is not problematic until the young boy is first confronted with the command to "act like a man"—typically around age three or four in our society. The boy is often at a loss to comprehend what this means. Grown men tend seldom to be present in the daily routine of childcare, so there are rarely any real-life role models available for boys to pattern a masculine identity after. The images of masculinity they are presented with tend to be unrealistic and unrealizable ideals of manhood (e.g., those portrayed by the mass media). To boys growing up in our culture, Rambo or Don Johnson may represent clearer images of masculine role models than their own real-life fathers simply because their fathers are not around enough for their sons to establish firm identifications with them. This sets up a dilemma for male children: They have an internal feminine identification, and they are faced with the external, somewhat elusive imperative to become masculine.

One typical way that boys resolve this dilemma is to define masculinity as whatever is *not* feminine. The little boy denies and represses whatever he takes to be feminine inside himself—those qualities he has internalized from his mother—and sets out to distinguish himself from her by accomplishing some feat he defines as masculine. Characteristic of these new "masculine" activities is that they *exclude* women.

Psychoanalysts argue that men never completely finish this "work" of achieving masculinity. The elusive, abstract way masculinity is defined in our society results in a kind of perpetual insecurity about it. Stoller, for example, discusses men's "need for constant vigilance against their unacceptable yearning to return to the merging of the symbiosis."[49] Their feminine tendencies pose a constant threat to men who are intent upon maintaining a masculine gender identity.

In this context, basic training performs a valuable psychic function for men who feel the need to separate and distinguish themselves from women. Marine Corps basic training promises to "make a man" out of new male recruits, who are often called "girls" until they prove their masculine prowess by performing feats set by the training regimen. Not unlike male initiation rites in other cultures, basic training marks off the difference between masculinity and femininity; it has been culturally defined as an activity only masculine males can accomplish. It unambiguously fulfills men's largely unconscious desires to prove once and for all that they are masculine.

The presence of women impoverishes these rites because it violates their raison d'être—to separate masculinity from femininity. If a woman can do it, the value of the ritual for proving masculinity is thrown into question. In other words, whenever men witness women accomplishing tasks they regard as masculine, their own masculinity is threatened.

This psychological dynamic sheds light on why military men seem so obsessed with preserving femininity among female recruits. Segregated training and policies requiring Women Marines to wear makeup and take poise classes are all veiled attempts to maintain the men's masculinity. Only if a clear distinction can be maintained between female and male marines can the masculinity of the Marine Corps remain intact.

Psychoanalysts note that males' denial and repression of femininity are often expressed in contempt for women. Men typically devalue whatever they consider feminine in order to minimize the feelings of loss that inevitably accompany the forced denial of their earliest attachment from childhood—the attachment to the mother. Men consider women inferior, weak, and incapable to ease their transition to a masculine identity. This is why Freud attributed a "triumphant contempt" for women to the masculine personality.[50]

This contempt for femininity is institutionalized in military policy. Segregation in basic training is mandated because men consider women incapable of achieving standards of military/ masculine performance—despite mounting evidence to the contrary. Allowing women in on an equal footing with men *appears to compromise* these standards in policymakers' eyes, whether or not the standards are actually compromised in fact, because they assume that women cannot achieve the high standards of masculine performance. To be feminine means to be substandard; it is not as good as being masculine.

Were the Marine Corps not so closely identified with masculinity, these psychological conflicts probably would not be as evident as they are. Other male-dominated occupations have begun to integrate without widespread fears about the manhood of the original male participants. What is more, the emotional desire to circumscribe women and maintain the masculinity of the military would remain *only* a desire were it not for the power that military men possess. Because men monopolize positions of authority in the Marine Corps, they can institutionalize these desires in official policy.

Official policies that discriminate against women have several serious repercussions on how their male colleagues treat women on the job. Because of the segregation of basic training, military women are an enigma to most servicemen. Male marines, when they are in leadership positions over the women (which is usually the case), often do not know *how* to evaluate or discipline them. A gunnery sergeant in the Marine Corps described what commonly happened when women integrated formerly all-male companies:

> At first, when we did away with [Women Marine companies], it was quite difficult because the men didn't want to discipline the women, didn't know how to correct them, with regard to their appearance; they just didn't know the regulations. And now [in drill instructor school] they are made to learn the regulations. I have to correct men; they should have to correct women. But there are still those out in the fleet who will come down to me and say, "Well, you talk to PFC Jane whatever about such-and-such because I am not comfortable with it." And I tell them to go take a flying leap, because she works for them. I take care of my people.

The results of men's ignorance about how to treat women can be rather benign: For example, women might get disciplined less frequently as a consequence. But there are more insidious aspects of this ignorance about women. Supervisors expect different performance from male and female soldiers based upon their beliefs about appropriate masculine and feminine behavior. Often these differences are drawn in a way that makes women seem inferior and inadequate. For example, a retired marine lieutenant colonel told me that when she underwent her yearly evaluation, one of the criteria she was judged on was "how well expected to perform in combat." She claimed her commanding officer had a very slanted and narrow view of what combat is: "To him it was crawling in the mud on your belly with a forty pound pack on your back." He did not take into account the extensive combat support that is required, much of which is administrative (her particular specialty). Thus, she was consistently underrated on this measure and, because of this, passed over for promotion.

Two other (enlisted) marines told me similar stories of being underrated on the criteria of "forcefulness," which they both contended was a euphemism for masculinity. Another marine told me she was marked down on her fitness report once because she was pregnant. Men in positions of authority over women often underrate them because they evaluate them on masculinity, a standard women can never measure up to.

Rosabeth Moss Kanter, who has studied the effects of token status on women who integrate all-male environments, calls this phenomenon "boundary heightening." She argues that members of a dominant group often exaggerate differences in response to the presence of tokens: "The presence of a token makes dominants more aware of what they have in common at the same time that it threatens that commonality. . . . Dominants thus tend to exaggerate both their commonality and the token's difference, moving to heighten boundaries of which previously they might not have been aware."[51]

The military is notorious for its use of misogynist imagery in basic training. New male recruits are called "ladies" or "girls" before they earn the derogatory appellation "boys." They march to sexist cadence ("I don't know but I've been told, Eskimo pussy is mighty cold"); and they learn about the dangers of acquiring venereal diseases from "Suzy Rottoncrotch." In the lounge of the student squadron where I interviewed female pilots, pictures of nude women and "Playboy" insignias were tacked on the walls. Women who enter the military—and particularly the Marine Corps—are stepping into an environment with deeply entrenched sexist traditions, and their presence seems to reaffirm these already "heightened" boundaries.

To begin with, female marines are never called simply marines. They are Women Marines (always capitalized) or just WM. They also have other unofficial nicknames: BAMs or Bammies (an acronym for "Broad-Assed Marines") and Marionettes. Male supervisors commonly call their female underlings by their first names instead of the appropriate use of rank title. A gunnery sergeant told me, "We have a lot of those [men] who want to call the women 'Suzy' or 'Terry,' and they call their male counterparts PFC So-and-so. That's not right. More women aren't letting them get away with that anymore." These names all "heighten" the differences between male and female marines.

Women in the services are often the subject of differential treatment on an informal basis as well as on an official basis. A recent graduate of the U.S. Air Force Academy described one dimension of this behavior:

> There was a lot of harassment of the women at the Academy. There was an image of women at the Academy which we had to fight against: big, husky, fat. You were always teased about that: "Watch out about your weight." . . . You hear it when one of the girls screws up—it makes us all look bad. If one girl is overweight, all girls are fat. Generalizations come fast.

Discrimination and harassment take several forms. One air force student pilot told me that her instructor came up to her and said, "You're not bad for a woman" after she had successfully completed a check ride in a supersonic jet airplane. Another air force woman told me that when she joined the service, her first boss told her, "I know why you joined the service: to find a husband and get married." Harassment is often even more direct: A Marine Corps survey of 615 first-term Women Marines reported that 13 percent were asked for sex in return for favors or threats of job action at least once.[52]

The differential treatment and harassment of military women continually create and maintain gender difference and militate against their acceptance as ordinary soldiers. Official policy as well as informal practices on the job constrain women's behavior and maintain the perception that servicewomen are inferior, marginal, or, at best, different from servicemen.

THE WOMEN WHO JOIN THE MARINES

Before arriving at the Women Marine Recruit Training Command at Parris Island, South Carolina, I was sure my image of basic training from films and popular stereotypes was an exaggeration. I quickly found out it was not. Drill instructors really do yell at errant privates for incredibly minor infractions. I learned this the hard way when a drill instructor yelled at me for crossing my legs while interviewing two "casuals." (Short for "casualties," "casuals" is the name given to dropouts.) Crossing legs is prohibited in the Marine Corps: One must always sit with knees together and both feet firmly on the floor. Luckily, I was able to explain who I was before being forced to endure I.P.T., incentive physical training, the traditional Marine Corps sanction of sit-ups or push-ups performed at the command of angry drill instructors.

Who in her right mind would subject herself to the punishing rituals of Marine Corps basic training? These young women had agreed to put themselves completely in the hands of apparently hostile and abusive drill instructors for over two months. Every minute of every hour of every day is regimented—they must even ask permission to use the bathroom. Women Marine recruits learn a new way to talk, stand, sit, and walk; not a single dimension of their personal bearing or mannerisms is left untouched by the training. After being on the island only a few hours, I knew I was dealing with a very unusual group of women.

But my experiences at Parris Island, and the dozens of interviews I conducted with recruits and drill instructors, convinced me that the women who join the Marine Corps are eminently "normal." The women I interviewed were articulate, reasonable people who, for the most part, joined the Marine Corps for realistic and responsible reasons. If anything, they are perhaps even more perspicacious about their futures than the eighteen- to twenty-four-year-olds I have met in my university classes.

The women who join the Marine Corps come from just about every race and ethnic group and a wide variety of class backgrounds. Blacks are overrepresented in the services; as Table 3 shows, almost 30 percent of all enlisted women are black. Many enlisted women have attended college; in fact, women in the military have higher educational attainments than women their age in the general population.[53] In the Marine Corps, 16.7 percent

Table 3.   Race/Ethnicity of Enlisted Women, 1983

	Department of Defense (%)	Army (%)	Navy (%)	Air Force (%)	Marines (%)
White	65.4	51.9	76.6	72.9	69.7
Black	28.3	41.8	17.7	20.4	23.7
Hispanic	3.1	2.9	3.1	3.3	4.1

Source: U.S. Department of Defense, Manpower Installations and Logistics, *Military Women in the Department of Defense,* 1984, pp. 104–5.

of the enlisted women have some college background, whereas only 6.7 percent of the enlisted male marines have ever attended college.[54]

Women who join the military generally do so for very pragmatic reasons. A 1978 survey of 2,553 enlisted men and women in the army found that men are more impulsive than women in their decision to enlist; that is, men considered this option for a much shorter time than women did. The study also notes that although both sexes are attracted to the military for the educational benefits, women generally have greater self-advancement motives than men. According to the report, enlisted women "tended to present a general enlistment configuration of more rational long-range planning, clarity of goals, goal direction, and higher personal aspirations than that of the men."[55]

Most of the women I interviewed said that a desire for financial security motivated them to join the military. For example, some entered because they had children to support. In economic terms, the military is an attractive employment option for many women. There is mandated "comparable worth" in the military—corporals make the same pay regardless of whether they are secretaries or machinists—and more favorable opportunities for advancement.[56] Many new Marine Corps recruits had been faced with the choice of joining the military or taking a sales job or other part-time work in the service industries. One recruit from the industrial Midwest, who had been a hairdresser before joining, saw the

Marine Corps as a steady 9-to-5 job: "It seemed, you can't get laid off if work got short—it was a guaranteed position, not like getting a job working as a secretary or computer programmer. The military doesn't lay off when things get hard. You always have your paycheck coming in. I wanted to go into a job where there was more security."

Emotional security is another reason many women enter the Marine Corps. Several felt the corps—with its relatively small size—offered the same sense of closeness and belonging often found in a large family. One private whose sister had also joined the marines described her own family to me: "There's three hundred relatives within thirty miles of where I live. We stick up for each other—we're not individuals. The Marine Corps is kind of like that. You stay by your own. It's like a big family. . . . And if something happens to me, they're going to take care of me."

Many women decided to join because they felt they were not yet ready or mature enough to assume an independent life away from home. A twenty-four-year-old sergeant reflected on her decision to join: "I was the only girl in the family. I had a very protective family. The Marine Corps was going to give me a chance to try out my wings. And I didn't have to worry about getting out of the house and falling flat on my face. It was a way of easing out of the house."

According to drill instructors, a sizeable number of women with backgrounds of family abuse join the services. One told me:

> Some come in because they're hungry. A lot of them haven't eaten in who knows how long. Some of them get molested at home, and they just want to get out of there. We correct them a lot, and I think it's for their own good, but a lot of them feel loved: "I have someone with me from sunup to sundown, and they care for me." A lot of the girls who come here have never been loved, and they've been thrown around.

The women who join the military are rarely motivated by a desire to defy traditional sex roles. (There are exceptions, called "Jayne Waynes" by other female marines.) My interviews confirmed the finding of the Marine Corps survey of first-term women in the marines on family plans and options for balancing family and career—that the overwhelming majority (95 percent) of female marines surveyed planned to marry and raise children. Approximately 80 percent planned to combine child rearing with their military careers.[57]

This is not to say, however, that the Marine Corps is a traditional career choice for women. The new female recruits share the common image of the Marine Corps as the most aggressive, tough, "masculine" branch of the military. As one told me,

> I chose the Marine Corps because I respect them the most.
>
> *Did you consider the masculine stereotype about the marines?*
>
> That may have been one of the reasons I chose the marines— because it seemed like it was so tough and high-charged. Most people picture a man in the Marine Corps. I still picture a man in dress blues when I think of the Marine Corps.

Many new recruits hadn't realized that women are allowed into the Marine Corps until their recruiters told them.

Women often cited the fact that the Marine Corps is even more male dominated than the other branches as a positive incentive to join: "That's one of the reasons I came in here: There's a lot of guys—3,600 plus to 1 ratio!" (The ratio is actually 24 to 1.) In fact, it was unusual to meet a recruit who didn't look forward to working around mostly males. An air force captain pointed out, "I think that the women who do go in generally have to like being around men. You know you're going to be surrounded by them."

How, then, do women conceive of their presence as women in this very masculine institution? I asked one private to compare a man in the marines, a woman in the marines, and a woman in the army:[58]

> The man marine is everything. He stands for marine: the ruggedness, that strength, the type of "go-get-'em." A Woman Marine retains her femininity, her identity as a woman, while also developing that bearing and everything else that goes into being a marine,

without losing her feminine, personal image. The army is like they're trying to make their women men.

What does it mean to retain femininity in the Marine Corps? How do the official policies of the Marine Corps and the informal daily practices that discriminate against women influence the meaning of femininity for these women? What are women's perceptions of their place in the service?

The first misconception about women in the Marine Corps that must be dispelled is that they are masculine. For the most part they value femininity and identify themselves as feminine. As one sergeant put it, "I'm a marine twenty-four hours a day, but I'm a woman *always*." Several women told me they had chosen the marines over the other services because it emphasizes the femininity of its female recruits more than other branches: "One thing I liked about the Marine Corps is that it's the only service that requires that you wear makeup during training. . . . I like that because it kind of symbolizes that they really want you to be feminine." But femininity means more to them than dress and grooming. The women I interviewed understand the difference between the rough-and-tough marine and the expression of femininity the corps expects of them: "You are in the marines, but they don't want you to lose the fact that you are female. They don't want you to act macho. . . . It's one thing they always want you to remember—you are a lady." What this means—to be a lady, to act like a "feminine marine"—was not obvious to me. When I asked them about this, the women could not articulate what it meant, although they agreed that it is an essential part of being a Woman Marine. A twenty-year-old recruit got tangled up in this ambiguity during our interview:

> They [the drill instructors] are always stressing when each is appropriate [the rough Marine Corps demeanor or femininity]. When marching in formation in our cammie greens [camouflage outfits], it's the hard type. When we are in our skirts, or out to dinner, or speaking with a superior officer, it's our feminine type. They just tell us when to use it and where to use it and how to use it.

What is the proper way to act when it's feminine?

It's military but. . . . It's a hard feminine style. It's hard to explain. Like when we're marching, the woman part drops out. It's just recruits out marching, slamming our heels down on the deck. When we're not in our cammies or out marching, it's put on your makeup and say yes or no, and don't bend down with your knees apart. I don't know, it's hard to explain, I'm having a hard time here. . . . The military's always there. . . . You're a woman at all times, but I guess there's times when you just let it shine out a bit more.

Do they teach you about this?

In etiquette classes, like when they teach you about going out to dinner or to the marine balls or even when we're just out on the town. We have to remember that we're marines, so we have to act feminine in a proper way.

I pursued the subject of femininity, asking my interviewees if they thought any type of woman would *not* be suited to join the Marine Corps. Their response? "The feminine, prissy type."

You still have a lot of women here who stand by on their femininity and get away with a lot of trash. It infuriates me.

Can you give me an example?

She's having her period; she's not going to empty the GI can. And they let them get away with it. The men scream and yell about how the women get rank much quicker—and I'm sure they do on the basis of their sex. Being nice and sweet. I've seen it, and it's not right. . . . There are some people who use their sex to get by, and they're succeeding because the men don't know how to handle it. Consequently, you have men who go overboard in the opposite direction and don't give women a chance.

This ambivalence—valuing femininity while disdaining it—is strikingly represented in an interview with a twenty-five-year-old drill instructor. When I asked her about the characteristics of new Marine Corps recruits, she said, "A lot of the recruits who come here don't wear makeup; they're tomboyish or athletic. A lot of them have the preconceived idea that going into the military means that they can still be a tomboy. They don't realize that you are a *Woman* Marine."

Drill instructors often bragged to me of their successes in turning new recruits into feminine women. Later in the interview, I asked this same drill instructor about the differences between working in an all-female environment (like Women Recruit Training Command) and an all-male environment, and what her preferences were. She said,

> I like being around men 'cause, if nothing else, it sharpens your feminine skills. . . . When you're around a man, you may be aggressive to a certain point, but there will also be times when you're going to turn on the charm to get what you want. If you need help doing something, if you need a favor, it's easier to get a favor from a man than a woman. It's not necessarily taking something from them. It's just using a bit of feminine charm. Not all women can do it.

Near the end of the interview when I asked if she believed there are any disadvantages to being a woman in the Marine Corps, she said:

> One thing that bothers me more than anything—in the service or elsewhere—is a woman who uses the fact that she's female to get over. Don't *use* the fact that you're feminine against what you're trying to accomplish. Don't use it to try to get out of things. I've seen it happen, and it disgusts me. I hate it. There's only eight thousand of us [Women Marines]. When one of us screws up, it can affect the opinion of fifty male marines. Every male marine she ever comes into contact with is always going to remember her. It will take ten good Women Marines to counteract it.

This interview illustrates the ambivalence surrounding the meaning and nature of femininity for women in the marines. This drill instructor encourages the development of femininity in her recruits, identifies with it herself, but then disparages evidence of it in others.

The key to understanding this contradictory attitude toward femininity lies in the various interpretations of what it means to *be* feminine that confront women in the military. Men and women have different ways of conceptualizing what it means to be feminine. Men in the Marine Corps have a negative attitude toward femininity: They consider women marginal to Marine Corps operation because they believe women are constitutionally incapable of performing the "masculine" feats required of full-fledged marines. But women in the marines value femininity. They believe a "feminine" woman is a self-respecting, dignified person worthy of special treatment. They consider army women, to whom they commonly compare themselves, "unfeminine"—undignified, "like men," and not meriting special treatment. Poise and personal appearance (makeup and grooming), as symbols of femininity, are also symbols of this dignity; thus, women do not object to rules requiring them to wear makeup or take poise classes: "The Marine Corps teaches women a more feminine way about the military. [*What do you mean by feminine?*] Well, a sense of pride in yourself, it builds up your confidence. . . . It's a finesse in the Marine Corps that's taught and stressed. . . . I'm talking about your personal appearance and how you carry yourself." Recruits said "feminine" drill instructors are their role models, describing them as quietly confident and deserving special respect.

For women in the marines, femininity does not inhere in a particular occupation. A Woman Marine can be a feminine drill instructor, machinist, or meat packer, possibly even a combat soldier. Femininity has more to do with a particular state of *being* than with actually *doing* anything, which points to an asymmetry in the meanings men and women attribute to femininity. The fact that men typically disparage femininity results from certain structural arrangements in the American family—most notably that women are the primary caretakers of children and are therefore the first persons with whom children identify. Boys are pressured to deny their attachments to their mothers at an early age and *prove* they are "masculine" by accomplishing specific tasks—by *doing* things. Feminine identity for the girl is consonant with her earliest childhood identification with her mother. What it means to be feminine is conflated with what it means to be human. Because self-identity and feminine identity develop concomitantly, there is no rupture in identity forced upon girls as there is for boys. For this reason, gender identity is less problematic for the girl; it is not something that has to be proven or achieved.

Thus, women in the marines do not feel that their femininity is threatened when they engage in "nonfeminine" activities. For them, the criteria for femininity are not one's accomplishments; femininity means self-confidence and self-respect—basic human qualities we tend not to associate with gender at all.

However, this is *not* what femininity means to male marines. To be feminine is to be inferior, a "sissy," not "up to snuff." That being feminine is incompatible with being a marine from the male policymakers' point of view is evident in the official policies of the Marine Corps: The reasons for excluding women from combat, segregating them in training, and requiring them to wear makeup are based upon the (male) notion that femininity means weakness, inferiority, or, at the very least, essential *difference* that disqualifies women from true and full membership in the marines. In fact, *the men* (not the women) perceive anything that sets women apart from them as incompatible with the military mission. And these differences are constituted by the policies affecting women and actively sought out via countless studies commissioned to "monitor women's progress."

This scenario poses an almost insurmountable dilemma for military women: They want to be accepted *as women* in a place where anything associated with being a woman is disparaged. And success in the military is contingent upon unquestioned obedience to the male policymakers' ordering of the organization—part of which is premised on the inferiority of women. Female marines internalize this masculine ideology to some extent insofar as they adopt Marine Corps values—for example, when they condemn other women for "using" their femininity to "get by." It is no wonder, therefore, that women in the marines show such marked ambivalence toward femininity. The source of this ambivalence is a very real conflict between their own feminine identification and what it means to them and the disparaging attitude toward femininity institutionalized in the military organization, which they also identify with.

In order to reconcile this ambivalence, Marine Corps women often interpret the discriminatory policies in a way that makes them compatible with their own positive evaluation of femininity. For example, many of the women I interviewed did not consider the different enlistment standards for men and women an instance of inequitable or discriminatory treatment. One recruit, after telling me that she had to score sixty to get into the reserves ("compared to forty or thirty for the men"), said, "They [the men] can be really dumb. I would like to see it [the entrance requirements] the same, but it lets you know that the women who are here are some of the best." Some women described women as the real brains behind the Marine Corps operation:

> Males can do basically anything. It doesn't take much smarts to fire a weapon. . . . Standards are higher for women. We're back for support, which means we've got to have a little more brains to do the paperwork, have the coordination to type and fix things like the artillery for the men. Whereas for the men you just basically send them out on the line.

Both of these women reconciled themselves to the military's discriminatory entrance policy by asserting women's *superiority* over men.

However, the different attitudes of men and women toward femininity were often reflected in the ambivalent ways women spoke of the special treatment they receive on the job:

> Sometimes on the job the men make you a center of attention by wanting to help you. *They think you're incapable or incompetent.* . . . A lot of times I've had a fight with the guys because . . . of things I wanted to do by myself, that I could do by myself. You try not to be rude, because sometimes you do really need their help. I think they do that because we're women. *But that's good.* It lets you know that gallantry is not dead. . . . What's the use of being a man or a

woman and not allowing yourself to conduct yourself so? I like to have the offer of help, because it lets you know that they knew you were a female.

Women Marines like men to acknowledge their "specialness," but at the same time they are suspicious about the basis for their special treatment. This makes them ambivalent about the differential treatment they receive from men.

To compound the problem, women realize that men often resent the special treatment women receive from other men. A sergeant in subsistence supply said this about her work:

> Forty to fifty pound boxes of meat had to be taken from the truck and stored. When I was assigned the job, often they would send over two male recruits to help with lifting. Some men resented that. This helped me do the job more efficiently—I could keep track of everything better—so it was to the benefit of my boss that that help was sent. But the men said, "If she's going to do that job, she should pick it up herself just like the males do."

This presents a proverbial "double bind" for women in the marines. They want to view men's special attention on the job as instances of gentlemanly courtesy and respect, even though they realize that others interpret this behavior as signs of their weakness or inadequacy. They often feel that they cannot turn down offers of help—even though they know such offers may get them in trouble down the road.

Experience of this double bind does not lead women in the marines to embrace feminism. On the contrary, several went to great lengths to distinguish their views from feminist ones. After describing the "sexist" attitudes prevalent among male marines, a lieutenant told me: "I think women ought to earn the respect in this field as well as elsewhere. Women should not expect men to give way just because there's women's rights. Women have to earn their respect." Another woman who had just told me that "men don't accept women—for pride or whatever" went on to say, "I don't feel inferior to anyone. Maybe it's the way you conduct yourself. Maybe they [feminists] don't like the way men treat them. If you don't like the way someone's treating you, then find a new friend. . . . I'm a firm believer that women bring things on themselves." The women I spoke to believe in equality of opportunity and responsibility, and they expect women to carry their own weight in the military. Yet they recognize that the Marine Corps does not treat women the same as men. A staff sergeant noted, "Some women are pampered. And when it's time to be strong with them, they break down in tears. They don't understand why the Women Marines break down like that. Women start thinking they deserve special treatment, and they don't."

One strategy female marines often use to mitigate this conflict is to "individualize" the problem: Many argue that discrimination is surmountable on an individual level. They view feminists and others who politicize their mistreatment as bitter women, incapable of standing up to the "challenge" of the Marine Corps. Those who are disgruntled about sexual discrimination apparently opt out of the corps, which is taken as evidence that these women are not cut out to "take the challenge."

Just how equal would women in the marines like to see the treatment they receive from the corps? I asked about their views on the segregation of basic training. Some opposed segregation; some favored it. In both cases, however, the basis for their opinions was their perceptions of how well the men would accept them.

> I prefer the integrated. . . . We should do things together like rappelling, so they can see what we do, and we can see what they do. A lot of the male recruits, they always say, "So, what do you guys do for training? It isn't as hard as ours." Our training is hard. Their training is hard for them because they're men, and ours is hard for us because we're women.

> Integrated basic training? Absolutely not. Women are not capable of undergoing all of the training that the men are. I think that it would breed contempt. The men would think that the women were getting equal pay and equal opportunity for fields and ranks,

and didn't have to endure near the trauma. . . . I think if you throw them all together, the kids are going to say, "Boy, them women, they're getting our quotas, they're getting our skills, they're getting promoted alongside of us, and their training is so much simpler than ours."

Segregation is important for recruits because of the distraction factor. An eighteen-year-old male marching behind a female isn't going to be thinking about what he's supposed to be thinking about.

Those who favored integration felt that women would be challenged to perform better in a competitive environment with men. Many who opposed integration felt the same way but recognized that women risk criticism and disparagement in a situation of direct competition: If they do worse than the men, they will be subject to contempt, and if they outperform the men, they will be resented:

Women and men are actually competing with each other. Women are trying to prove themselves; even though sometimes they don't have to, they still are. They want to show everyone, "Hey, look, women can be in the marines. We're not that bad; we know what we're doing. We're not that bad—accept us!" And the male marines are doing what they can to make it look like they're better than the Women Marines, that they still stand out.

The women I interviewed about the combat exclusionary policies expressed the same trepidations about complete equality. Women Marines are apparently very split on the issue of women in combat: Fifty-four percent of the women surveyed by the Marine Corps said they either might or would definitely volunteer for combat if it were possible.[59] However, all but two of the women I interviewed said they would definitely go if they were called upon to fight.[60] What did these women think about the combat exclusionary policies?

There is apparent unanimity among those opposing the combat restriction policies as to the reasons for excluding women. They believe the policies were instituted *not* because of women's trepidations about entering combat zones or physical or emotional incapacity to deal with the rigors of combat, but rather because of male inability to accept them in these areas:

> I think it would be hard to put women in combat. Because of the way society raises men and women differently—for the men to protect the women. There's going to be too many casualties. If you have a man and a woman together in a foxhole, he's going to wait for her out of pure chivalry, or being male, or being brought up in our society. And he'll wind up getting them both killed.

As I noted earlier, the air force women I interviewed were most vehement in their opposition to the policies excluding them from combat. I asked one instructor pilot why, in her opinion, women are barred from flying fighter aircraft. She replied,

> They don't want the women in POW camps—and I can understand that—but I think that if a woman realizes that she can be shot down and raped every day in a POW camp, and she's willing to take that chance to defend her country just like everyone else does, she should have that right. . . . Most of that argument comes from my peers. Not that they don't think I can handle it; their argument is that if we got shot down together, and they're interrogating me, and brought him in and beat me because I wasn't answering, then the man would be more apt to say something because I'm a woman, and they don't want to see me beaten because of them. I can understand that. But what if it's reversed, and they bring in someone and beat him because I'm not talking. If they start beating up any human being, you're going to want to spill your guts. So I don't buy that argument. I tell them this, and they say, "Well, I was raised that way." Well, that's just a growing pain.

The women I interviewed for the most part agreed that the segregation of basic training and the combat exclusionary policies are based on men's attitudes toward women and their inability to accept women as colleagues in defense. Many of the women who claimed they would fight if called upon to do so accept the restrictive policies:

> I believe that women cannot handle themselves under that much stress. If they allowed us to go in [to combat], all they'd be doing is

killing half our population. I believe that only one out of five or six women will be able to shoot back if someone is shooting at them. They would just freeze under pressure and forget how to pull the trigger, forget how to load the weapon.

How about yourself?

I believe I could handle it. I love shooting weapons. . . . I've always been a real tough go-getter. I myself could handle it because I've always been really good under stress. And I could pretty much outdo any other guy in the same situation.

This contradiction between declaring a readiness to fight and believing that women are not capable of fighting came up again and again:

There are a lot of women who would like to join the infantry and the closed specialties. I would love to be in the infantry—to be a grunt. It's just my nature. I am just really motivated to serve in the Marine Corps. I would do anything for them. There are a lot of people who feel that way. We understand why we're not allowed to.

Why?

It's more of a male role. There are just too many limitations on us, a woman, as far as the body goes. I don't think we could handle it out there. We could handle it mentally and physically, but not really, if you know what I mean.

No, I don't understand.

Personal things. I don't think women could be out there like in Vietnam for a year straight, going without food, and the hygiene part of it. Plus having our feminine role. We're there to back the men up.

Many of the women I interviewed expressed this ambivalence toward femininity. These young recruits accepted the grounds for their exclusion from combat—women are inferior to men, they break down under pressure, they're physically unfit to endure the rigors of fighting. To some extent, they have co-opted the Marine Corps' negative evaluation of femininity. Yet at the same time they insist that *they* are personally capable of meeting the demands

of combat. By viewing herself as an exception to a general rule—
"women are incompetent, but I am not"—a woman can resolve
the contradiction between men's negative evaluation of femininity
and her own positive sense of self-worth. This strategy accommo-
dates women to the restrictive policies without diminishing their
sense of their own abilities and individual prowess. This accounts
for women being able to put up with the unequal, discriminatory
treatment they receive at the hands of men even though, in princi-
ple, they are opposed to discrimination.

Although for female marines "feminine" describes a dignified,
confident woman worthy of respect and special treatment, male
marines disparage femininity because it means inferiority relative
to masculinity. Women's attitudes toward femininity actually accommodate themselves to men's negative evaluation. When faced
with special treatment from men, women usually interpret it favorably, as an instance of warranted respect. The notion that they
deserve special treatment is gratifying on some level; female marines are to some extent flattered by men's attention and constant
notice. Those who object to this treatment are considered hostile
and bitter by their peers because, by refusing to accept this interpretation of men's behavior toward women, these women challenge the very grounds for other women's acceptance of the status
quo.

What would happen if women recognized that they are kept
out of combat, forced to wear makeup, and subject to constant
surveillance in the form of studies because of men's negative evaluation of femininity? Their ability to remain in the military would
be severely undermined. This is precisely what happens to women
who give political meaning to their special treatment: They opt
out of the services. This indicates to the women who stay that they
were not able to take the challenge of the Marine Corps, which
again vindicates the belief that those who stay are special, meriting
special treatment.

I am not claiming that women in the marines have an inaccu-
rate or invalid understanding of what femininity is; I believe that

their definition of femininity and their appreciation of the various gratifications associated with it are entirely valid. Recognizing these positive gratifications does, however, help us understand why women accept practices that, upon closer inspection, are based on negative and derogatory views of femininity. Women do not accede to discriminatory policies because they are masochistic or consider themselves deserving of punishment. Rather, they for the most part interpret these policies in ways that reflect favorably upon themselves as women.

Of course, there is another reason for women's adoption of official military policies: They have no alternative if they want to stay in the Marine Corps, where men have all the power. Promotion and advancement are contingent upon following orders that filter through a set hierarchy of command.

Men control the reigns of the military, so in the last instance, their evaluation of femininity is the most significant in determining policy toward women. As long as the military is associated with masculinity, and as long as men need to believe that women are incapable of performing specific "masculine" feats, they will continue to exclude them, regardless of what women are actually capable of achieving. For this reason, the outlook for further sexual integration in the military remains bleak.

4

Masculinity in Nursing

Opportunities for men nurses have expanded tremendously during recent years. Avenues which once were closed have opened wide. Now the registered man nurse is eligible for the Nurse Corps of the military services as a Reserve Commissioned Officer. The U.S. Public Health Service has openings for him. Veterans Administration hospitals find his services invaluable. Industry needs him in mines, foundries, and in construction work. Personnel on psychiatric wards wonder how they ever got along without him. More than ever is he in demand in the field of anesthesia and for the care of men patients with fractures, heart disease, and genitourinary conditions.

Textbook on nursing history (1959)[1]

There is a smaller proportion of men employed in nursing than in any other profession. Male nurses have never reached 4 percent of all nurses; in 1980 there were only 45,060 male nurses in the entire United States (see Table 4). There are indications that male nurses will make up a slightly larger percentage of the profession in the future. Table 5 points out that the percentage of male nursing students has been increasing since 1962.

Why are there so few men in nursing? Few formal barriers stand in the way of men who wish to practice nursing today. In this chapter I examine the obstacles that existed in the past, focusing specifically on the military's exclusion of men from the nursing corps. The military's refusal to accept male nurses prior to 1955 arose from the concerns of military *men;* women in the nursing establishment supported those male nurses who fought to join the corps. In Chapter 3 I indicated how military officials' desires to maintain gender results in the inequitable treatment of female soldiers. Here

Table 4.   Number of Male Nurses in Selected Years, Compared
to All Nurses

Year	Number of Registered Nurses	Number of Male Registered Nurses	%
1980	1,662,382	45,060	2.7
1978	1,375,208	27,301	2.0
1972	1,127,657	14,625	1.3
1966	909,131	8,227	0.9

Sources: American Nurses' Association, *Facts About Nursing, 82–83* (Kansas City, Mo.: American Nurses' Association, 1983), p. 10; American Nurses' Association, *Inventory of Registered Nurses, 1977–1978* (Kansas City, Mo.: American Nurses' Association, 1981), pp. 126–27; American Nurses' Association, *Facts About Nursing 76–77* (Kansas City, Mo.: American Nurses Association, 1977), p. 14; American Nurses' Association, *Facts About Nursing 70–71* (Kansas City, Mo.: American Nurses' Association, 1971), p. 17.

Table 5.   Men in All Registered Nurse Programs

Year	First-Year Enrollment (%)	Graduation (%)
1962–63	1.7	1.2
1965–66	1.8	1.7
1968–69	3.5	2.2
1971–72	6.1	3.8
1974–75	6.9	6.1
1977–78	6.3	5.5
1980–81	6.4	5.2

Source: U.S. Department of Health and Human Services, Public Health Service, *Minorities and Women in the Health Fields* (Washington, D.C.: Government Printing Office, 1984), pp. 162–63.

I show that in the past male nurses were also subjected to exclusionary policies designed to reaffirm gender boundaries.

If there are presently no formal barriers to men's practice of nursing, what then accounts for their dramatic underrepresentation in the field? Could it be that men are pushed out of nursing by the medical and nursing establishments? I examine the treatment of male nurses by their female colleagues, by physicians, and by patients and others outside of the hospital. Informal workplace pressures tend to marginalize male nurses or, more accurately, to distinguish their contributions from those of female nurses. The male nurse is treated as an enigma in the hospital. However, by and large such distinctions do not *negatively* sanction men interested in the practice of nursing. In fact, the differential treatment of male and female nurses often *benefits* men in nursing, giving them greater prestige and more autonomy.

The major reason there are not more men in nursing has nothing to do with either legal restrictions or institutionalized practices. There are few men in nursing because *men do not want to be nurses,* and those who are express strong ambivalence toward their chosen profession. The male nurses I spoke to went to great lengths to distinguish what they do from the traditional conception of nursing tasks. Some men choose to enhance their technical nursing skills; others specialize in administration. The bedside nurse emphasizes his nonnurturing functions, such as his physical strength, allowing him to pick up and move patients. Men use such strategies to demarcate and distinguish their contributions to nursing from women's role in the profession. I argue that the men perceive an immense pressure to stake out a terrain within nursing to identify as masculine because the profession is so closely associated with femininity.

In the final portion of this chapter, I discuss the motivations of the men who decide to enter nursing and explore several of these "masculine strategies" they use to legitimate their presence within the field.

The picture that emerges of men in the female-dominated world of nursing is compatible with the psychoanalytic account of masculinity discussed in the previous chapter. Male nurses, like male marines, have the emotional need to separate masculinity and femininity, which is part and parcel of sustaining a masculine gender identity. This goal of separation often takes the form of hostility toward women: It is not uncommon for male nurses to blame women for the lowly status of the profession and to criticize their "feminine" attitudes toward physicians. In these practices male nurses are similar to the male marines I described previously.

However, unlike military men, men in nursing do not monopolize positions of power. Although they are overrepresented in administrative ranks, they do not control the profession. The struggle to maintain masculinity is for them a private, individual one: Nursing has no mandated segregation that defines certain specialties as masculine, as does the military (e.g., combat billets). The interviews that follow reveal the men's idiosyncratic efforts to carve a personal niche for themselves, thus allowing them to maintain masculinity in nursing.

NURSING LAW

Prior to World War II, men had only limited opportunities to study nursing in this country. In 1941, there were sixty-eight American coeducational nursing schools (out of a total of 1,303) and four schools that accepted only male students.[2] Most of the schools that admitted men were affiliated with mental hospitals and trained psychiatric nurses. At that time the curriculum for psychiatric nursing was substantially different from that of general nursing. It came under the auspices of the Medico-Psychological (later the American Psychiatric) Association, unlike general nursing, which had a much broader base. The result, according to historian Mary Roberts, was that there was little overlap between the training of most male and most female nurses: "Psychiatric nursing was quite outside the experience of the majority of nurses who participated in the early development of the professional nursing organizations. There was, therefore, no common bond of interest between most of the men and the majority of women nurses."[3] Added to this segregation was the popular practice of calling male nurses "attendants" instead of "nurses."[4]

During World War II, there was a practical hiatus on the education of men in nursing. One of the men-only schools stopped admitting new students; another closed down entirely. Between 1945 and 1948, the largest number of men to graduate in any one year was forty-two.[5] During this period, male nurses lobbied unsuccessfully for military deferments and for assignment into the Army and Navy Nursing Corps. These efforts continued unabated after the war, and legislation that would have permitted men to join the nursing corps was introduced on two subsequent occasions, only to die in committee hearings.

According to Roberts, many male World War II veterans wanted to use the GI Bill to study nursing after the war.[6] Schools slowly began to open their doors to them: In 1948, there were 115 coeducational nursing schools; in 1950, there were 183.[7] A study commissioned by the New York State Nurses Association in 1948 found that the chief obstacle to admitting more male students was lack of adequate housing facilities—not inadequate demand. (During this period, most nursing education took place in hospitals that boarded students.)[8] This new influx of men inspired the National League for Nursing Education to recommend in 1950 that there be no differentiation in the basic curriculum for male and female nursing students.[9]

Yet not until 1955 was legislation to permit men into the military nursing corps finally approved. The congressional hearings on H.R. 2559, the bill to permit men into the nursing corps on reserve officer status, provide some insight into what was then considered the appropriate role for men in nursing and their anticipated contribution to the military. Representative Frances Payne Bolton (D-Ohio) spearheaded the drive to pass H.R. 2559. Speaking on behalf of the male nurses, she testified:

> We felt for a very long time that it was a great waste of vital manpower, for there are some nursing jobs for which men are best fitted. Psychiatry, combat assignments, and so on, are among them. . . . This bill would provide a group of Reserve officers for whom there is much demand in both war and peace. At all times, they will fill a great need in psychiatric wards of hospitals and other

specialized wards and in assignments really exacting too much of women. In time of war, they could be very literally in the front line.[10]

A psychiatrist speaking for the American Psychiatric Association pointed out that half of all patients hospitalized in the United States were in mental institutions—evidence of the enormous need for male nurses. In support of his argument that male nurses were better suited for work in psychiatric hospitals, this psychiatrist, who was chairman of the committee of psychiatric nursing of the American Psychiatric Association, said:

> [Psychiatric] patients are sometimes assaultive, sometimes make persistent attempts at escaping; they may tend to take off their clothing, may be over erotic and sexually perverse; sometimes their toilet habits have deteriorated, they are untidy and filthy. They may need to be controlled by physical force, and the nursing personnel on the wards are sometimes exposed to dangerous attacks. Not only this, but mental illness is characterized by difficult emotional problems of interpersonal relationships, and it is not at all uncommon for men patients to be extremely hostile toward women.[11]

He argued that the army could increase the general supply of male nurses by opening the doors of the nursing corps to them:

> The attitude of the Armed Forces has actively interferred [sic] with the motivation for men to go into nursing. At the time the young man is considering his future trade or profession he is brought face to face with the need for putting some time in the military service of his country. At this time, he finds out that the military does not recognize that men can be graduate nurses. If he is not very strongly inspired to go into nursing this tends to discourage him, and he is thus lost to the profession.[12]

A representative of the American Nurses' Association made one final point on behalf of male nurses, arguing that, despite their small number, male nurses could potentially replace *all* female nurses in combat areas during wartime:

> Although the percentage of men nurses in the total active professional nurse population of the United States is relatively low, 2.4

percent, this represents 9,613 men registered nurses, a sizable reservoir. The potential of available personnel in this great number is greater than it would be in a like number of women nurses since women with dependents under 18 years of age cannot be recruited into service. Nor can women remain in the corps following motherhood. This problem does not exist for the men in the services.[13]

The bill passed unanimously and was signed into law in August 1955.

These House hearings reveal the conditional nature of men's acceptance into military nursing. Supporters of men in nursing justified their admission into the corps by arguing that men's qualifications differ substantially from women's. Rather than usurping women's role, men were reclaiming an area of nursing practice for which they were inherently better suited. The underlying sentiment was that female nurses should never have been permitted to perform some of the nursing duties they had been assigned during the war—particularly service near the front lines of combat.[14] Combat and psychiatric nursing were considered "men's work," so only men should have been doing it. An additional argument was that men posed fewer administrative problems because they were not subject to the rules governing female nurses regarding marriage and children. The justice of these regulations was not questioned. Indeed, advocates for the male nurses argued that the rules would be easier to enforce once men replaced women in military nursing.

Thus, the establishment of gender distinctions was key to gaining acceptance for men in nursing. As a result, the integration of the nursing corps was accomplished without any challenge to occupational sex segregation.

Once the military agreed to accept male nurses, few *legal* obstacles remained for men in nursing. One of them, state support for nursing schools that excluded men, was successfully challenged in 1982 when the Supreme Court ruled that this practice discriminated against men.[15] The major barriers to the full integration of the profession are no longer legal ones.

In the previous chapter, I argued that the status of women in the military is constrained by official exclusionary policies. The result of these policies is that women are concentrated in administrative specialties and overrepresented in the lower ranks. Although there are no legal barriers to men in nursing, they, too, tend to be concentrated in certain specializations and overrepresented in certain "ranks" within the nursing hierarchy.

In nursing, as in other female-dominated occupations, men are concentrated in the most prestigious and best paying specialties.[16] Men tend to gravitate toward acute care, intensive care, and psychiatric nursing. That men were previously denied training in obstetrics and gynecological nursing and pediatrics may account for their overrepresentation in other areas, and they continue to face limited opportunities to practice these specialties in certain parts of the country. (Hospitals set their own policies, which vary regionally and by private affiliation. For example, Catholic hospitals tend to be more conservative on this issue.) In recent years male nurses have challenged hospitals in court for these exclusionary policies and have generally been successful.[17] It is unusual to find any such formal barriers in place today.

Male nurses in general earn a higher median income than female nurses. In 1981, the median income for men in the profession was $17,888, compared with a median income of $16,952 for female nurses.[18] Part of this income discrepancy can be attributed to the concentration of men in the higher paying specialties. More significant, however, is the overrepresentation of male nurses in the higher administrative *ranks* within nursing (Table 6). There are proportionately more men in administrative positions in nursing than women and proportionately fewer men in general ward duty nursing, which could account for the salary discrepancy between men and women. However, recent research by Janet Gans suggests that men make more money even when they occupy the same positions as women. Gans found that male nursing directors earn on average $1,500 more per year than female nursing directors.[19] Yet her study, based on a national survey of 5,052 nurs-

Table 6.   Male and Female Nurses by Type of Position, 1980

	Male (%)	Female (%)
Administrator or Assistant	6.0	4.8
Consultant	1.0	0.6
Supervisor or Assistant	5.9	7.7
Instructor	3.2	4.8
Head Nurse or Assistant	4.7	7.2
Staff or General Duty	59.2	65.0
Nurse Associate/Practitioner	1.8	1.3
Clinical Specialist (Master's Degree)	2.6	1.5
Nurse Anesthetist	9.4	0.9

Source: American Nurses' Association, *Facts About Nursing, 84–85* (Kansas City, Mo.: American Nurses' Association, 1985), pp. 25–26.

ing directors, reveals that educational attainment—not sex—is the most significant variable in explaining this salary discrepancy. Almost 40 percent of the male directors in her sample had completed postgraduate degrees, compared to only 25 percent of the female directors. When she controlled for education, this salary discrepancy vanished.

It is true that male nurses as a group have more advanced degrees than female nurses (Table 7). Thus, men as a group make higher salaries because they are better credentialed than female nurses. According to Gans, education is overall the best predictor of career success in nursing. Table 8 presents the distribution of first-year students in the three most popular entry-level registered nurse programs. The associate degree in nursing, a two-year program that leads to the registered nurse certification, is currently the most popular program for both men and women. Proportionately more women than men attend hospital schools of nursing (three-year programs awarding a diploma instead of a university degree). Twenty years ago, the diploma schools were the most popular programs among nursing students; now they are gradually being phased out. Approximately equal proportions of male and female nursing students opt for the four-year, university-

Table 7.   Male and Female Nurses by Highest Educational Preparation, 1977–78

	Male (%)	Female (%)
Diploma	35.4	59.8
Associate Degree	28.6	12.2
B.S. in Nursing	17.2	15.0
Bachelor's Degree in Another Field	9.5	3.1
M.S. in Nursing	2.7	2.4
Master's Degree in Another Field	3.2	1.4
Doctorate	0.7	0.2

Source: American Nurses' Association, *Inventory of Registered Nurses 1977–1978* (Kansas City, Mo.: American Nurses' Association, 1981), pp. 126–27.

Table 8.   Men and Women Enrolled as First-Year Students in Entry-Level RN Nursing Programs, 1981

	Men (%)	Women (%)
Bachelor's Degree	30.2	31.8
Associate Degree	56.7	51.5
Hospital Diploma	13.1	16.8
Total	100.0	100.0

Source: U.S. Department of Health and Human Services, Public Health Service, *Minorities and Women in the Health Fields* (Washington, D.C.: Government Printing Office, 1984), p. 162.

based baccalaureate degree in nursing. All three programs lead to the same registered nurse certification.

Gans discovered certain structural forces that give men an advantage over women in their pursuit of higher education. Controlling for marital status, she found no difference in the educational attainment of married and unmarried male nurses, but married female nurses are significantly less likely than unmarried female nurses to pursue advanced degrees.[20] This can be attributed to the fact that married women in our society bear most of the responsibility for household care and child rearing even when they are employed outside the home.[21] Thus, marriage is a career liability for female nurses because it limits their opportunities to pursue advanced education.

After granting the male-female discrepancy in educational attainment, Gans concludes that it is unjustifiable to claim that men are unfairly advantaged in the nursing profession. But perhaps more intriguing is her finding that men as a group are *not* disadvantaged or subject to discrimination in nursing, which contradicts the theoretical claim that minority status itself results in discriminatory hiring and promotion practices within organizations.[22] Despite their numerical underrepresentation, men do not encounter institutionalized or formal barriers to their advancement within nursing.

In the previous chapter I discussed several informal military practices that contribute to the marginalization of women. I introduced Kanter's theory of tokenism to account for both the increased performance pressures placed on female soldiers and the phenomenon of boundary heightening that adversely affect the acceptance of women into the regular military. I also argued that Kanter's theory of numerical rarity in organizations offers a plausible explanation for the informal marginalization of women in the military.

Men in the nursing profession, like women in the marines, are subject to special treatment on an informal basis. Indeed, the phenomena Kanter associates with tokenism are also evident for men in nursing. However, the etiology and the consequences of these phenomena differ for these groups of male and female tokens. In the case of male nurses, it is the *men* who attempt to construct boundaries separating themselves from their female majority.

Past research on female nurses' attitudes toward men in nursing indicates that, in general, they welcome the entrance of men into the nursing profession. Gans's in-depth interview study of 25 male and 25 female nurses concludes, "In general, women encourage, support, and promote men in nursing to a greater degree than they support other women."[23] McCarragher, who surveyed the attitudes of 87 male nurses and 147 female nurses in the Ohio

Nursing Association, found overwhelming support for the man in nursing: About 81 percent of the women surveyed agreed with the statement, "The nursing profession should encourage the entry of more men" (compared to 88 percent of the men).[24] This study replicated a 1976 New York State study of 126 female nurses that also concluded that the majority of female nurses have a positive attitude toward the man in nursing.[25]

This isn't to say, however, that men are *treated* equally by women in the nursing profession. To begin with, in nursing school men experience what is apparently a common experience of all minority groups in organizations: They stand out and are noticed more by their instructors and fellow students. A male senior in a bachelor's of science in nursing (BSN) program told me:

> I think I've been noticed more easily because there's ninety people in our year, and eight guys. So I know for a fact that I'm visible. . . . I especially remember going in to talk to one professor who had never met me face to face, but he heard of me. . . . That recognition aspect must make a difference. You go up to talk to a teacher, and they know who they're talking to.

With a few notable exceptions, nursing educators are enthusiastic and supportive of their male students. One thirty-eight-year-old nurse who entered an associate degree in nursing (ADN) program after several years working as a military corpsman and hospital orderly recalled his experiences in school in 1973:

> I was encouraged from square one. The lady who was the director of the nursing program . . . was encouraging, as were most of the educators, to any man who was seriously interested in becoming an RN. In fact, she was pushing us both [himself and the other male student in his class] to go on and get our master's and teach, do legislative work, or some other pertinent nurse-advocate work.

Another man, a 1978 BSN graduate, said of his schooling: "There were six men in the class of forty students. They wanted to keep men in the program. It wasn't like they were helping me, or tutoring me along. But I got encouraging words from a lot of the instructors. . . . Some of the instructors I worked with on the clinical rotation would say, 'There is a need for men in nursing.' "

It is not unusual for instructors to encourage their male students to go beyond the general nursing degree and pursue graduate education. An instructor in a BSN program recalled: "At my first counseling session in my nursing program, I was told, being a male, I should pursue a master's program when I graduated." He was also channeled into administration and nursing education by his instructors:

> At that time there was a lot more stereotyping about what areas in nursing men should and should not go into. I do remember that I really liked peeds [pediatrics], and that's where I wanted to work when I graduated. I went to a peeds instructor—she was kind of the department head—and she advised me very strongly that that was not a place for men to work. So being young and naive . . . and not even realizing that that was a form of discrimination, I did not go into peeds. . . . Back then I think men were socialized to work in more acceptable areas, like OR [operating room], psychiatric nursing, or urology.

In some cases men report that female nurses feel threatened or otherwise have expressed ambivalence toward them. It was not uncommon to hear from the men that some female nurses resented the fact that they accelerate faster in their nursing careers than women. One student nurse, the president of a student nurse organization, told me: "I think men have it easier, to tell you the truth . . . and women hate us because of it. It's like we're treading on their turf, and we get all the glory. I've encountered a lot of resistance on the part of women." This feeling was echoed by a male doctor of nursing science (DNS) who directs a BSN program:

> I think the women in nursing are very ambivalent about men in nursing because there have traditionally been so few options for women to get ahead. In nursing, a woman can be in administration, or director of a hospital, or dean; whereas most of the deans in the other departments will be men. So when I've applied for

positions, several times I've been qualified, and I've been told that it would be the kiss of death to make that university appointment because they have so few opportunities to appoint women.

Thus, men in nursing find encouragement and support from the majority of female nurses. But the fact that they may use this support to their career advantage apparently frustrates many female nurses and causes some to express resentment toward the men.

Female nurses also have informal ways to set men apart in the daily practice of nursing, the most widespread being the allocation of lifting assignments. Male nurses are called upon to do an inordinate share of lifting and stevedoring of patients. These comments from male nurses are typical:

> I worked at a convalescent home for about four months. It was really hard work, taking care of geriatric patients. I was the only guy there, and I was like a forklift, picking people up off the floor all the time. I messed my back up there.

> I feel as though I've been given special consideration for being a man in nursing. I think some of it centers around a need for someone who can tolerate heavy lifting. . . . A lot of my cohorts who are women, particularly those who are under 150 pounds, are not physically capable of coping with lifting.

> We [male nurses] tend to be used for real physical things. "Help me move this patient." "Help me get him into this wheelchair." Physical kind of stuff.

In addition to being used to lift and transfer patients, male nurses are often called upon by their female colleagues to assist them in certain procedures with male patients:

> If you really want to catch the attitude of sexism in nursing, it's on the issue of catheterization. I'm just as skilled to do either [a male or a female catheterization]. I've done more men because they call me, even when it's not my case. In fact, after I quit the state hospital, I became an orderly in a community hospital in intensive care. They called me all over the house if they had a difficult male catheterization.

One additional activity of female nurses serves to alienate men from nurses generally: Male nurses are often excluded from the socializing networks of their female co-workers. When Liliane Floge and Deborah Merrill observed over 540 hours of nurses' interactions in two small northeastern hospitals, they found that male nurses were often absent from women's informal socializing groups:

> Observations indicated that the typical conversations of female nurses revolved around such "female" topics as baby and bridal showers, finding a man, their husbands' sexual habits and sexual needs, various aspects of the female menstrual cycle, giving birth and raising children, boyfriends' and husbands' habits, clothing and haircuts. Male nurses were not included in these conversations and the female nurses made no attempts to include them. . . . It was only when the female nurses were not discussing such female oriented subjects that male nurses were included, although there were several instances in which men were not included even in gender neutral conversations. There were many social events in which male nurses were not included. One hospital had a female nurse's softball team. Male nurses were not invited to lingerie parties, tupperware parties, and houseware parties; yet these were the only parties that the nurses had. In addition, there were very few friendships between male and female nurses.[26]

The men in my study did not mention such exclusion, although several noted that they conscientiously avoided involvement in any such "girl talk."

In sum, men believe that female nurses are generally supportive of their presence in nursing, and several studies on women's attitudes toward male nurses corroborate this finding. One of the reasons for this support may be the widespread perception that an increase in the number of men in nursing may enhance the status and prestige of the profession and increase salaries. Officials of the American Nurses' Association argued recently in Equal Employment Opportunity Commission hearings that excluding men from nursing has resulted in depressed wages.[27] Several of the men and women I interviewed also mentioned this possibility.

Some men perceive resentment toward them on the part of female nurses in the upper echelons of the nursing hierarchy. I have no data from female nurses either supporting or disputing this claim, but men do seem to advance faster in the profession, which could fuel women's fears that they are taking over their career ladders.[28] Although Gans's study suggests that this faster pace of promotion is due to factors other than sex, it is not surprising that some women might conclude that men are favored for promotion on this basis.

One thing is certain: The American Nurses' Association's *official* position is that men should not be discriminated against in any way by the nursing profession, and this has been their policy for many years.

There is a general consensus among male nurses that physicians treat them better than their female colleagues. To begin with, they believe that doctors are more likely to listen to their advice. These comments are typical:

> It is my opinion that doctors respect the intelligence and judgment of the man nurse more readily, in that a female nurse may have to "prove" herself before she gets this respect; whereas the man is more likely to receive it from the start.

> Doctors relate to me better [than to female nurses]. Just as in a man-to-man relationship. . . . They don't want to be thumbing through catalogs and looking at fashions. They want to be talking about golf.

One male nursing student, assigned to interview nurses and physicians as part of a student project, said,

> I had one doctor tell me that he was glad to see more men go into nursing because they were more decisive. He said that to my face, and didn't see that there would be anything weird about saying it. That's the least inflammatory of what people brought back [from this assignment]. Some talked about how they liked the sexual tension between the male doctors and the female nurses! It's just mind-boggling.

By many accounts, verbal and physical harassment of female nurses by physicians is not an uncommon occurrence. Several of the men I interviewed noted this harassment:

Do doctors treat male and female nurses differently?

Oh, yes. They can't slap our butts. They can't put their arms around us and make sexual jokes and comments. Some of it is joking and kidding; some of it is sexual harassment, but they can't do that to us.

Very often both male and female physicians treat me with more respect. They do not regress to childlike behavior of shouting, yelling, throwing things (charts) when something doesn't go as ordered. I would not tolerate this and would make a direct comment about the behavior.

In December 1985, I attended a meeting of the American Assembly for Men in Nursing. At a seminar session on male nurses as a minority group, the discussion leader asked the twelve male nurses whether a physician had ever thrown anything at them (e.g., charts, medication, scalpels). Two said this had happened to them. When asked whether they had ever witnessed this behavior directed at a female nurse, every man present agreed this was a common occurrence. The male nurses I interviewed escaped or avoided the abuse that often characterizes the doctor–nurse relationship.

Physicians' special treatment of male nurses may enhance their chances for promotion. Floge and Merrill found that physicians' evaluations of nurses indirectly determine nurses' positions in hospitals.[29] The fact that the doctors in their study perceived male nurses as more competent than female nurses influenced the promotion of male nurses to higher positions in the hospitals.

The exception to the generally favorable treatment of male nurses by doctors may be the case of older physicians, who apparently have more difficulty accepting men in nursing: "Some physicians would rather relate to female nurses. . . . Your old-fashioned physician who is used to being the big boss, who is very hierarchical and authoritarian, is going to say men shouldn't be in nursing; it should be all females."

Many men told me that they enjoyed working with female physicians, noting a frequent measure of empathic understanding that results from their shared "outsider" status: "I personally love working with female physicians, although I like working with my male colleagues as physicians as well. . . . This society is still extremely sexist, and it will be for a long time to come. Female physicians tend to be much more aware of that sexism . . . so their level of acceptance is much better. Also, they're struggling, too."

In general, then, my research did not confirm the expectation that male nurses would be negatively sanctioned or suffer from lack of acceptance by physicians in their daily practice of nursing. Whatever special treatment the male nurses do receive seems to enhance their careers, not detract from them.

Male nurses encounter the most "mixed" responses when they come into contact with people outside the medical establishment. Perhaps the most common misconception about them is that they are in training to be doctors. One student nurse told me: "When I was working at Children's Hospital, you wear scrub uniforms like they wear in surgery. . . . People would be confused and think you were a medical student and start addressing you as a doctor, and you'd have to say, 'No, no, no, I'm just a nurse.' " One nurse told me that even members of his family believe he's really a doctor: "A lot of people think I'm a doctor. My family always comes to me for medical advice. They even have friends of theirs come and ask me advice: 'Come over here. Carl has a little spot on him; come look at it.' " Even when patients recognize that male nurses are not doctors, they commonly assume that the men *wanted* to be doctors but couldn't make it. A male assistant professor of nursing told me: "Most people will still say, 'Gee, why don't you become a doctor?' or 'Didn't you want to become a doctor?' "

Situations in which patients refuse care by a male nurse sometimes arise. One told me a story of an older European woman who refused to be given a bedpan by him, saying, "No man should handle a woman's dirt." So he was forced to find a female replacement for this duty. This reaction is most common in obstetrics and gynecology wards:

> *Have your patients ever been surprised when you told them that you were their nurse?*
>
> One time when I did encounter it was in the clinic with this antepartum. . . . They were doing Pap smears, and the nurse practitioner there would ask the patient if it were all right for a male nurse to observe the procedure, and I had several who turned me down. . . . That's the only time I encountered prejudice.

Often, however, the source of uneasiness is not women patients, but their *husbands:* "I've noticed some uncomfortability with some husbands who bring their wives in. I come in, I introduce myself, and they look at me. . . . Their wives are going along with the program, but they're very tentative and want to know everything that you're doing."

"Dear Abby," a syndicated newspaper column, ran a series of letters about men in nursing in 1985. The following excerpts from two of them illustrate the caliber of prejudice male nurses sometimes encounter in the performance of their duties:

> DEAR ABBY: You asked your readers how they felt about male nurses. Well, let me tell you. If I caught a male nurse tending my wife, he would leave her room faster than he went in. Men should stay in man's [sic] work, or confine their nursing to men only.
>
> DEAR ABBY: If I ever have to go to a hospital, I will give strict orders not to send me a male nurse to even give me a bedpan. (I would sooner be looked after by the cleaning woman.) . . . If a man wants to be a nurse, let him find a job in a veterans hospital.

However, the rejection that male nurses sometimes face may be countered by patients who prefer having men care for them:

> A lot of times men like to be taken care of by men, and also there's a lot of times that women would rather be taken care of by men, too. . . . Several times I've found that to be true in my practice:

There's women who really appreciate being taken care of by a man. I've had men say to me, "I really feel embarrassed taking off my pajama bottoms for a female nurse."

A student nurse shared this view:

When I worked at the veteran's hospital . . . there were very few female patients, and most of the people I dealt with were older men. In some situations, I feel it was easier for me than for my female colleagues. . . . I think that old stereotype of wanting a pretty nurse around you . . . there is some truth to that. These men may want a pretty nurse. But in some situations, they may be more comfortable with me around.

Thus, just as there are situations in which patients *refuse* care by a male nurse, they sometimes seem to *prefer* being cared for by a man. Overall, the male nurses I spoke to reported a positive level of acceptance by their patients.

Another popular stereotype about male nurses is that they are all gay. Nurses encounter this stereotype both at work and in their private lives: "There was a stigma about it when I was in corps school: Men in nursing were considered fruits. There were a lot of gay men. . . . That's still a problem. I've had several women [nurses] approach me in the emergency room and say, 'Are you gay?' Straight out. . . . It's like an assumption." Another man said, when I asked him why he thought there are so few men in nursing, "I think it's because of the stereotype. This is more my own stereotype when I went in—men get labeled being gay or not as masculine when they go into nursing. . . . This is a man's world, and men have always been brought up not to be sissies or anything that's related to female job qualifications." When I asked twenty-five male nurses the question, "What do you believe are the major barriers to the inclusion of more men in nursing?" on an open-ended survey questionnaire, fifteen answered that the social stigma associated with entering a feminine profession is a major barrier. Part of this stigma is the implicit assumption that men interested in nursing are homosexual.

Another aspect of the stigma placed on male nurses concerns the practice of nursing itself. Male nurses told me that it was not uncommon for others to regard nursing practice with scorn or even disgust: "I think generally people think, 'Why is he in nursing?' . . . Sometimes they assume that there's something wrong with me. They don't know what to say. A lot of them say, 'Gee, I don't think I could do that.' They right away see the giant bedpan and all the cleaning up [a nurse has to do]." I interviewed one female nurse who said this about the stigma facing her male colleagues:

> It takes a special kind of man to go into nursing. . . . I remember being at a party . . . with mostly male attorneys. Three of them said, "I'll dig ditches before I do that kind of stuff" [referring to nursing]. And these are people who pride themselves on being liberal! First of all, it's insulting to me. But they only think it's insulting when you're talking about their own sex doing it. . . . They made comments like, "Not only do you have to shovel shit, you have to smile when you do it." . . . We're never going to have to worry about having a lot of men in nursing.

The low status of nurses generally may be exacerbated in the case of men. For instance, many told me that their parents had been disappointed when they first told them they had decided to enter nursing, a problem women probably would not encounter as frequently:

> When I graduated from high school, I said I wanted to be an anesthesiologist and go to medical school. My father said, "Great." And he just happened to say, "But don't become a nurse." As part of the praise of congratulations, he just threw that in. . . . He thought I was too good to be a nurse. Coming from a better background, and having too much up here, he thought I was just going to waste it.

Another man said: "My parents never explicitly said, 'Why don't you become a doctor instead of a nurse?' But I remember getting this sense that they thought that nursing was not shooting far enough. . . . I got this sense that nursing is not quite as challenging or rewarding as other stuff I might have done." One male nurse confided that he wouldn't want his own son to enter nursing. When I told him that this surprised me, especially because he was on the board of directors of a nursing organization, he argued that his was a common view. He pointed out that when women enter nontraditional professions—such as engineering or medicine—parents are generally pleased because these are high-status professions. But when men enter what have traditionally been women's fields—such as hairdressing or nursing—the reaction is not as favorable. There is a *loss* of status in the latter case.

Certain informal practices distinguish men from the lot of nurses generally. Their female colleagues, doctors and patients, and friends and family "remind" male nurses of their renegade status. This "special" treatment generally results in favorable prospects for the male nurse's career: He is treated with more respect than female nurses, encouraged to seek higher education, and channeled into the most prestigious specializations. Receiving unfavorable evaluations of his performance or being considered unsuitable for nursing because of his sex rarely has any direct bearing on a man's career advancement. In other words, the fact that some patients may refuse care from a male nurse or that someone at a party would disparage the choice of nursing as a profession has little impact on the male's status within nursing. However, this is not true for homosexual male nurses. Rumors of homosexuality may diminish a man's prospects for promotion. Men in nursing must individually come to terms with the negative sanctions they receive.

THE MEN WHO BECOME
REGISTERED NURSES

Why would any normal man ever choose to become a nurse? Few have done so: In 1980, there were just over 45,000 registered male nurses in the entire country. With so many other employment options available to them, why would any man enter this female-dominated, underpaid, and relatively low status profession?

Psychologists have asked this question under the guise of personality research that seeks to determine whether men in nursing are more "feminine" than other men.[30] These studies used psychological testing devices to conclude that there are no significant personality differences between male nurses and other men.

Like women who join the military, men who enter nursing generally do so for pragmatic reasons that rarely have anything to do with a desire to defy traditional sex roles. A 1963 attitude survey of 516 male nurses and nursing students found that the reason men gave most frequently for choosing nursing as a career was "Because I like people, and enjoy helping them," followed by "I wanted to go into medicine but was financially unable to do so."[31] Other responses to this question emphasized the desire for financial security.

Other researchers have replicated this study, albeit with much smaller samples. In 1976, Garvin studied survey questionnaire returns from thirty-four male nursing students and found that medicine was their most seriously considered alternative career. She hypothesized that the men who choose nursing over medicine tend to come from working-class backgrounds and therefore lack the resources to fund medical school educations.[32] Evidence does suggest that the majority of male nurses come from working-class backgrounds.[33]

Several of the men I interviewed told me they had entered nursing because they could not afford to go to medical school. Others, who had come to nursing rather late in life, said they had considered going to medical school but had felt they were already too old to embark on ten years of training. One man with military corpsman experience explained why at age twenty-seven he had opted for a two-year nursing program over medical school:

> [After my hospital corpsman experience] I wanted to work critical care, and I didn't feel 100 percent sure that I could get through a premed course. I didn't want to make that commitment of time. I felt at that time it was still possible for me to do it—but by the time I got through med school and paid off my loans, I would be in my

forties. I didn't feel I had enough active career time left to warrant
going and making the effort.

One man, who lacked the "time, money, and A's" to get into
medical school, compared his nursing education to the rigors of
medical school. He said that nursing school "was a lot harder than
I expected. The way they ran it, you ate, drank, and breathed it.
When I look at the interns here [at the hospital where he now
works], I put myself in their position. We were up at 5 A.M. to be
in surgery; then we had to go to class; back to the hospital to
work patients—it was very hard." For him, medical and nursing
schools offered comparable training. A senior in a bachelor's program had a similar attitude toward medical school. When I asked
him how his family had reacted to his decision to become a nurse,
he said,

> My mother always wanted me to be a doctor. . . . I think there's a
> certain amount of disappointment in that respect.
>
> *Had you ever considered becoming a doctor?*
>
> Not really. It never was a financial possibility from my angle to go
> to medical school.
>
> *Was it ever an interest?*
>
> Well, it wasn't directly. Certainly since I've been in nursing, I've
> thought about it. . . . I think it's something that I probably could
> have managed. Or even have done a better job compared to some
> of these jerks I see as medical students.

The fact that so many people question male nurses about why
they did not become doctors often results in an attitude of defensiveness. One joked that he hadn't become a doctor because "I
can't play golf." Others were more philosophical:

> *Did you ever consider becoming a doctor?*
>
> Yeah, I thought about it. . . . For one thing, I really didn't want to
> go through med school. . . . I have sort of a negative image of
> doctors as a social and political force. I have great respect for a
> good doctor, but I feel that socially they've completely blown their

claim to respect because of all these abuses of power. . . . They've forfeited their claim to sensitivity, and staked it all on diagnosis. There's aspects of that kind of medicine that I find really negative. So I didn't want to do what I thought doctors did. . . . I didn't want to be linked with them as a member of that class.

Thus, there may be some truth to the popular assumption that some male nurses at least *considered* becoming a physician before becoming a nurse.

Many men mentioned job security and financial incentives when I asked what motivated them to enter nursing. One student nurse said,

There was this great demand for nurses. . . . You could get hired absolutely anywhere. You could sometimes get jobs where you would just work two twelve-hour shifts on the weekend and get paid the equivalent of working a forty-hour week. The same benefits. There was such a shortage that the benefits that the hospitals were offering were tremendous.

Another man told me that nursing attracted him because he thought it would lead to quick promotion and easy advancement: "A couple of things encouraged me then. One of them, which is a myth, is that when you're a nurse, you're always going to have work. . . . But the other thing I heard was that if you're a man in nursing, doors open to you all the time. Which, in a sense, was kind of true."

Male nursing students tend to be older on average than their female counterparts.[34] Whereas girls commonly consider becoming a nurse early in their lives—usually before age fifteen—boys usually do not view nursing as a possible career until much later. A 1968 study of 506 high school boys found that nursing was their least likely choice of occupation.[35]

When men do enter nursing, it is usually *not* directly after high school but after some hospital or other medical setting experience. Of the thirty-four male nurses I interviewed and surveyed, twenty-six reported prior hospital experience—as an orderly, corpsman, or some other auxiliary occupation.

Some men simply fell into nursing for lack of alternatives. This was usually the case for men raised in rural communities that housed state mental institutions. One man raised in a rural area, whose brother is also a nurse, explained how they became involved in the field: "We were in an area where there were three businesses: aerospace industry, agriculture, and the hospital. I think it was because my older brother is a quadriplegic that both of us fell into doing medical care. Opportunities presented themselves. Also, nursing didn't cost me a dime; the state paid for it."

The older men I talked to had attended sex-segregated nursing programs that had separate administrations for male and female nurses. They said it was not at all unusual for men in their rural communities to enter nursing. One man, whose parents were both psych technicians in the state mental hospital, described the networks of families employed by the institution:

> Families who lived in the area were three generational. The grandparents may have been psych technicians and pushed all their kids into nursing school because they knew they weren't getting ahead. And they didn't differentiate whether they were boys or girls. . . . I found a similar situation when I went to work in consultation at the state hospital, when I had students there. It was so similar— these maps of families were three generational, too, and they had long roots.

These men's decisions to enter nursing were not at all incongruent with their identifications with masculine roles. Because there were equal numbers of male and female role models at the hospitals, and because the duties of the sexes were clearly delineated (men generally specialized in psychiatric nursing and urology with male patients), nursing did not have an exclusively feminine connotation. For the majority of men in the profession today, however, nursing is closely associated with a feminine calling.

I have noted that male nurses tend to be concentrated in the acute care specialties, administration, and psychiatric nursing. When I asked one man why he preferred acute care, he said,

> I didn't want to take a job on the med-surgical floor, which means anything other than emergency room, operating room, or intensive care unit. That means just the place where you pass bedpans, doing bed care. In ICU, you're dealing with intensity, death sometimes. There's always something there to keep you excited. I like the pressure; I need something to do. I just can't go with the mellow, mothering types of things of a floor nurse.

Several of the men I interviewed disparaged the lot of the general duty ward nurse and sought out acute care specializations for their technological aspects. One explained why he first became interested in nursing: "I think at that time I was more interested in technical things, all the gadgets, intravenous therapy, suction, respirators, telemetry. . . . And I thought, boy, this is really high-tech, and I really enjoyed it."

Male nurses also say they find the acute care specialties and psychiatric nursing attractive because they give the nurse either more autonomy (psychiatric nursing) or closer collaboration with the physician. A student nurse said this about why he plans to practice nursing in emergency room settings:

> In some of these intensive care situations, the decisions you have to make about changing the levels of various drugs the patients are receiving at the time are really really critical decisions. One slip up and you kill somebody. . . . In those kinds of situations is where you find the most mutual respect between doctors and nurses, where there's more of a recognition that we're colleagues in a way.

Psychiatric nursing calls upon practitioners' strength to restrain and subdue violent patients. Presumed to be better equipped physically and psychologically for dealing with such patients, male nurses are drawn to this specialty. When I asked one nurse why he thought there are so many male nurses in psychiatric units, he said, "That's purely the physical dynamics of having someone who's crazy and strong around that you occasionally have to wrestle down to the ground. There are times when people are so psychotic that if you're a woman, they're still going to smash your face in. That sounds ridiculous, but it's really true. So they really want guys in nursing."

My respondents often said that male and female nurses are suited for different specialties. As one male student nurse stated:

I never saw one male nurse that worked in either labor and delivery or postpartum, or in the nursery. That's not exactly true; there were a number of men who worked in the intensive care nursery for premature babies. There you have these two-pound babies with all sorts of tubes and lines coming out of them, and you just sit over this baby the entire shift, watching this bank of monitors. That's a very technical kind of nursing, so there were men in that area. But not in the other areas. I don't necessarily think that that's bad or that it should be changed. It just seems that there are certain things that women are more comfortable doing, and having another woman dealing with them in that respect. I think that men can be good nurses, and be in most all of the areas, but there are differences between the sexes which might as well be acknowledged.

Thus, the stratification within the profession is often justified on the grounds that men and women bring unique abilities with them to the practice of nursing.

The final significant dimension of the specialties that men gravitate toward is that they all have less distinctive dress than characterizes nursing in general. Nurses in acute care settings wear scrub uniforms (which often leads patients to presume they are physicians); nurses in administration and psychiatry wear normal street clothes.

Thus, in a variety of ways, the men's choice of specialization helps them distinguish themselves from the lot of nurses in general and enables them to define their work in terms of a traditional masculine sex role. That is, the stratification of the profession maintains masculinity within a feminine profession.

How do male nurses respond to the special treatment they receive from their female colleagues, physicians, patients, and those outside the hospital? In general, the men I talked to conceded that their female peers accept their presence in nursing. How do they respond to the special tasks they are called upon to perform? Many men mentioned that they are given an inordinate share of lifting assignments when I asked them if they ever feel subject to discrimination. However, my probing into this issue clarified that lifting is *not* a task they hate or avoid, but is rather a source of job satisfaction for many. One man, with nineteen years of nursing experience, said, "There's a lot of stevedoring in nursing. Nurses have never been given credit for the fact that they have to do rough, heavy work. It just goes with the territory, and the risk of injury is very great." I then asked him whether he resents being called upon to shoulder most of the heavy lifting assignments. He said,

> They [female nurses] want me and expect me to do the heavy lifting. And I like that; I like that relationship, because I don't particularly want to do the pelvic exams. If we can make that trade, the patient needing the pelvic exam is more comfortable; I'm more comfortable transporting patients, and I know they're not hurting their backs.

This man's view that male nurses make an important contribution to nursing because of their superior physical strength was held by many of the men I interviewed. One man added that this asset of physical strength distinguishes the type of care male and female nurses provide:

> Men have the capacity to care—I think it's definitely in a different way—but they have the capacity to care for people. Women show their caring to a person who is dying one way; I think men have a different way of doing that.

> *Can you describe the difference of caring?*

> I don't see little details, but I see the main things I need to do. One thing I always liked to do for [this one lady who was dying of cancer] was to help her lie comfortably. I'm strong, I can lift her, I can put her in a position where she's comfortable in bed. . . . And the women focus on different things. . . . I wouldn't put makeup on somebody. Or take care of somebody's hair the way they like it. But a girl knows how to take care of another girl's hair because

they're used to it. But I don't take care of another guy's hair. . . . I'm also good at massaging and doing ranges of motions for them . . . and she really appreciated that. Those are the different kinds of things that I would think of. . . . I think the two work well together.

What is interesting about the issue of lifting and physical strength is that it is an attribute of masculinity that men used to explain their role within nursing to me. Men—quite consciously—distinguish themselves from female nurses with their willingness to perform heavy lifting assignments. In a sense, therefore, they are as complicit as women (perhaps even more so) in defining these tasks as masculine and thereby carving out a special niche for themselves within the profession.

I detected a similar phenomenon in an interview with a senior nursing student. We were discussing his training in obstetrics and gynecology. When I asked him whether he ever felt uncomfortable in that setting, he said,

There was a funny thing that happened, before we ever went into the clinical. The woman coordinator of that clinical was lecturing to a class of mainly women: "You're going to be going into these women's rooms, and they just had a baby. You're going to be feeling their breasts; you're going to be feeling their bottoms. Some of you may never have felt a woman's bottom before." I had to bite my tongue! Because in that sense, I had probably dealt with women's bodies more in a certain way than a lot of women have. I thought it was really ironic that she said that.

This man felt strongly that biology was no grounds for excluding men from the practice of obstetrics: Men in fact could be seen as *more* competent in "dealing with women's bodies" than women were. He thus redefined the quintessentially feminine purview of obstetrical nursing in a way that valued "masculine" (and, more specifically, masculine heterosexual) experience.

As I pointed out earlier, male nurses are not as integrated as female nurses into the informal work environment—friendship networks. Floge and Merrill suggest that this is because men are *ex-*

cluded from informal socializing among nurses.[36] On the contrary, my interview research indicates that men exclude themselves from this socializing—an important distinction. Many men I talked to felt a need to distance themselves from the private concerns of their female colleagues. A senior nursing student explained: "I'm around women all the time. I feel like I need to sort of escape from that a certain while and be with my male friends and do male things. You know, like go down to the garage and work on my motorcycle and get my hands dirty. Talk about motorcycles or something like that. Just to reestablish a little bit of balance." At the convention of the American Assembly for Men in Nursing, I asked several men why the organization is important to them. The typical answer was that it provides the opportunity to be around other male nurses. At a discussion session on men in nursing as a minority, one man said, referring to his male and female colleagues, "You're able to joke with a guy, but with a woman you don't talk the same language. . . . It's nice to share things with men. You have a professional attitude towards both, but when it comes to small talk . . . the women only want to talk about babies and periods. [Everyone laughed.]" The men said they sometimes engage in this small talk—they aren't excluded from participating—but they don't enjoy talking about these things all the time. Another nurse told me: "Sometimes I feel weird being around women all the time at work. If they've had a rotten few relationships, all day long they're going to rag on men. . . . Sometimes by the end of the day, I'll get involved in one of their discussions, angrily, and say, 'You can't say that about all men!' "

The men said they prefer to talk about sports and vehicles, which also happens to be the preferred small talk among (male) physicians. The nurse who told me that doctors relate better to him than to his female colleagues because doctors want to talk about golf—not fashions—noted,

> That's a problem because I don't want to talk to them excessively and alienate the female nurses. . . . The doctors will gravitate to-

wards me, and I don't want to spend an excessive time with them. . . . A couple in the emergency room are building boats [a hobby of his], and they want to talk boats with me excessively, so it's disruptive. . . . It's rough to turn them off because you have to work with them, too, and they act insulted if you're not interested in what they're saying.

This segregation of small talk involves two factors. On the one hand, the men themselves are deciding not to engage in the informal conversations of female nurses at the workplace; they are not intentionally excluded from participating. In this regard, men are again segregating themselves from the lot of nurses in general. On the other hand, male nurses are pressured by male physicians to engage in small talk with them. This also serves as a mechanism for maintaining gender segregation in the workplace. Thus, the special treatment that male nurses receive regarding both the allocation of lifting assignments and the exclusion from informal discussion at the workplace to a large extent originates with the male nurses themselves.

How do the male nurses come to terms with the ambivalent treatment they receive from patients and people outside the hospital? Many told me they have difficulty getting patients to accept the fact that they are really nurses: Patients—especially children— often insist on calling them "doctor" in spite of their explanations. At the other extreme, some patients make a big issue out of the fact that they are male nurses. One man told me his patients frequently ask, "How do you like male nursing?"—a source of aggravation to him.

I found that male nurses generally have two responses to being turned away by patients because of their sex. Some argue the patient has a right to refuse treatment. Being turned away does not detract from men's overall contribution to the profession because there are other contexts in which female nurses might also be turned away because of their sex (male catheterization, for example).

Others are angered by what they feel is, in this instance, discrimination. Some told me that men should be allowed to practice in all departments of the hospital, including obstetrics and gynecology. After all, one man argued, most doctors, including gynecologists, are men. Another man told me he was so frustrated by patients' trepidations about letting him care for them that he was finally pushed into acute care settings:

> It bothers me when people say,"The male nurse came and helped me." The term "male nurse" is demeaning. . . . The distinction does not need to be made. . . . What happens is, in petty situations, where a woman is in for having a mole removed, I'm not going to go into her room and try to do anything with her or for her. If the woman's bleeding to death, or her heart stops, and her husband is at the bedside, he's going to be kissing my feet and glad that there's someone in there taking good care. So that's kind of why I work in the intensive care unit—the differences [between men and women] are stripped down to the basics.

Male nurses are aware that they're stigmatized as effeminate. Choice of specialty can be seen as a strategy to minimize the stigma of being male in a female profession.

This may be another reason why many avoid general ward duty nursing and why some describe the type of care they provide as different from that female nurses provide. For example, a nursing administrator explained,

> I think men demonstrate nurturance and caring to the same degree as a female would, but the demonstration of it is different. I don't think we always touch as frequently and say soft, kind words. I think my caring is of the same depth and degree, but it's more overt than covert. It's not warm fluffy; it's different. Some might even say that's not really caring or nurturing.

By distinguishing the type of care he gives, the male nurse carves for himself a separate niche within the profession that allows him to maintain his masculinity within a feminine context.

There is a pervasive stereotype that all men in nursing are homosexual. Most men I interviewed and surveyed identified this as a major barrier to the entrance of men into the profession.

Those who entered nursing were forced to confront their personal misgivings about the sexuality of men in feminine occupations. A senior nursing student recalled his early trepidations about the field:

Did you have any trepidations about entering nursing because there are so many women in it?

Just slightly. . . . When I was in school in some of my other classes, and people would ask what my major was, the first couple of years I was hesitant. I would always go, "I'm in the health field." . . . I wouldn't feel shameful, just a little hesitant. People associate nursing with gayness, and I didn't want labels or anything. But right now I could say it without hesitation. It's still slight, but very slight.

Male nurses develop various personal strategies for coping with the stereotype of homosexuality. Some use specialty choice to avoid labels of effeminacy and homosexuality: The acute care specialties and psychiatric nursing require little intimate personal contact with patients and provide few contexts for accusations of sexual impropriety on the job. General ward duty nurses downplay the nurturing aspects of their jobs, emphasizing the physical strength required of them and their professional technical training. These strategies help not only to distance them from female nurses, but also to avoid the stigma of homosexuality.

Many nurses I interviewed went to great lengths to affirm their heterosexuality to me. This information was always volunteered; no question in my interview schedule addressed the respondents' sexuality. One male nurse who wrote in response to the "Dear Abby" column mentioned before said in his letter, "So here I stand, heterosexual and proud to be a nurse and a man." As far as I can tell, none of the previous letters in the column suggested that male nurses *weren't* heterosexual. (Most assumed that male nurses were lecherous with female patients.) Straight male nurses seem to be overly defensive about their sexuality, whether or not it has been openly challenged.

These straight men's acceptance of homosexuality in others

varied considerably. Some apparently did not care that there are gay men in nursing; others were antagonistic toward gay men for perpetuating the stereotype and thereby keeping more men out of nursing. In general, however, the men I interviewed believed that most men in nursing are *not* homosexual and that the incidence of homosexuality matches proportionately its incidence in the wider population.

The exception to this is the city of San Francisco, popularly considered a gay "mecca." This area also has a large number of male nurses, above the national average. Many people believe these two phenomena are related. That is, they believe that many of the male nurses in the city are drawn from the large homosexual subculture.[37]

The gay male nurses I interviewed had been drawn to nursing in part out of concerns related to their homosexuality. The treatment of acquired immune deficiency syndrome (AIDS) was a central issue for them. One man told me he believed that the majority of male nurses working in the AIDS clinics are gay.

Another nurse who identified himself as homosexual to me in the course of the interview said that, for him, being gay was more of an issue than being male in the nursing profession: "Out here [in San Francisco] it seems that men [nurses] do not tend to get promoted faster than women. I think that has to do with the large gay population—I'm not sure that doesn't enter into administrative selections. It's taken a lot of time for gay men who are quite skilled to get into administrative positions." The discrimination he witnessed against men in nursing was based more often on prejudice against homosexuality than on prejudice against men per se.

This is an added incentive for straight males to *emphasize* their heterosexuality. In the military hospital corps especially, there is a danger of immediate dismissal if homosexuality is discovered. One man with navy corpsman experience recalled: "There were a few gay corpsmen who were weeded out by the navy very abruptly. It was sad, because some of the things I thought were not just; the guys weren't necessarily gay."

On the issue of sexuality, it was a common view that the man in nursing—homosexual or heterosexual—must be secure about his sexual identity. I asked one nursing student if he believed there is a type of man who would be unsuited for nursing. He said,

> Certainly if you have a lot of hangups about your own sexuality, and your own identifications being a man, if you're straight. . . . Usually, the gay men don't have that problem, "What am I doing in this female occupation?" But for straight men, if you have a problem about it, you better straighten that out before you start working because that may be a problem identifying yourself as a nurse.

I asked another nurse if he thought the negative stereotypes about men in nursing are diminishing. He said, "I think it's going away, but there are a lot of gay men in nursing. And so there's still going to be a little of that stigma attached to it. For those who are straight in the profession, they have to have strength of character enough to shirk it off. I am straight, and the other men I know in the emergency room are straight." The stereotypes of homosexuality are so pervasive that men feel pressured to constantly assert—and defend—their sexuality. As another male nurse said, "You're gay 'til proven otherwise."

The picture that emerges of male nurses' responses to the special treatment they receive from others is a mixed one. Although male nurses are treated differently than women in a variety of ways, the men themselves are instrumental in perpetuating and maintaining those differences. By emphasizing their unique sense of caring, their special (physical) abilities, and their distinct personal interests, the male nurses set themselves off from female nurses and attempt to distance themselves from any association with homosexuality. Remarkably, this same act of "distancing" can be detected in men's attitudes toward the profession of nursing itself.

I asked all the men I interviewed and surveyed how they see themselves in the future with regard to nursing. Of the thirty-four who responded, three said they would no longer be involved in nursing. The rest said they would be employed in administration, teaching, acute care, or private practice (with a nurse practitioner license). Of the ten students and men currently employed in ward duty nursing, not one planned to work predominantly as a bedside nurse in the future.

The men I talked to generally viewed nursing as a "springboard" to other professions. As one said, "When I got into nursing, it was never meant to be the end. It was meant to be a rung on the ladder." Several men shared his views: "Nursing is definitely a diving board [to other careers]. I think it's so in some sense because nursing has never been reinforced for men as a lifelong profession."[38]

Why don't men want to stay in nursing? One of the most common reasons is low pay. One nurse said,

> Since I've been married, I've wished I was in a profession where I could make more money. I love nursing, I really do, but it doesn't have enough money for me. . . . Lately, I've been thinking about applying to pharmaceutical companies to see about a position where I would sell their hospital products. . . . That would keep me in contact with nursing, but it would also bring me into the business profession, which kind of interests me.

Equally important as low pay, however, is the low status of the profession, which also "pushes" men out. Here's what one nurse said when I asked him to describe what he would be doing in the next five to ten years:

> I will be struggling like a dog to get out of nursing. Most definitely. . . . Where's to go in nursing? What am I supposed to do? I can't make any money. I'd like to get married. I'm not gay—I'm totally straight. . . . I want to get married and afford a nice house and have some power and some respect. . . . I just don't see any respect for nursing, and I don't see any financial rewards. . . . It bothers me that checkers can make $13 per hour, and nurses who are making comparable wages are literally responsible for people's

lives, and having to give medications that you're legally responsible for. . . . I don't need that kind of stress unless they're going to take care of me in return.

This man has become frustrated with the profession because he has not received the payback from nursing he feels he deserves. He believes his responsibilities are just as great, and his work just as demanding, as physicians'; yet his financial rewards are a fraction of doctors' incomes. Thus, the pressure to socialize and identify with physicians that I described previously can have adverse consequences for men in nursing. If they identify too closely with physicians, men may become disenchanted with nursing because of its relatively low status and low pay.

The men who specialize or take administrative positions are also seeking to escape the low status of nursing. A director of nursing at a major urban hospital said this about his profession:

> Nurses have more responsibility than just about anybody else in the hospital. . . . We have the responsibility of twenty-four hours taking care of these people. But nurses still do not make one-third the salary that physicians do. . . . Fifty percent of the people who graduate from nursing school will leave nursing within two years. . . .[39] They burn out. They say, "Why am I putting up with this? I have skills that I can go on and work in almost any other industry, doing just about anything else, and make as much as I do now and not have to be put down all the time."

As director of nursing with 160 people working under him and with more schooling than many doctors (he has a Ph.D. in nursing), this man has *made himself* a colleague of physicians in the hospital, thereby overcoming the subservient relationship between doctor and nurse.

The issue of low status is often raised in discussions about affirmative action. Some argue that nursing ought to aggressively recruit men for openings in nursing schools and take steps to ensure equal representation of male nurses at all levels of the nursing hierarchy. This is a divisive issue among men in nursing, with strong sentiments both ways. One advocate of affirmative action argued that increasing numbers of men in the profession would "increase pay, improve hours, and increase the respect" of the profession, thus benefiting both men and women. Others took a critical view of this policy. A student nurse said that affirmative action in nursing

> would be promoting people to lower status. . . . In this case, it's men going into something that has traditionally been lower class, lower status, lower power. So what are you going to do, force people into something that is seen that way? When you talk about affirmative action to be firemen, policemen, all that, it's a step up. But for men, nursing is a step down still.

In both cases, the argument centers on the low status of the nursing profession. Both sides recognize this as a problem, but their strategies to address it differ.

What is the cause of the low status of nursing? Here the men spoke with a unanimous voice: The problem with nursing is that it is a woman's profession. In fact, many men argued that nursing suffers from low pay and low status because women in general are not assertive enough to force hospitals to recognize their contributions to health care. When I asked one man what he thought would have to happen for nursing to gain more respect, he said,

> Women will have to fight and stick up for who they are and what they do, and women do not do that. So many times women in nursing do not support themselves, for one thing; more likely they tear each other apart. . . . I don't think women are strong enough, they're not vocal enough, they're not demanding enough. I'm sure that men are more demanding and will be over the years. You just can't treat men that way and get away with it. Women have allowed themselves to be treated that way, and it's just self-perpetuated.

This argument is not at all unusual. The authors of a recent article on men in nursing contend that male nurses could teach female nurses to be more aggressive and demanding:

> Psychological testing generally portrays males as self-confident and self-assured during the preschool years. During the midchildhood years . . . play activities are aggressive and team- or club-oriented.

Male adolescents show increased bravado and expansiveness. . . . Therefore, it should be natural that men would bring these attributes to the profession of nursing. . . . It is logical to assume that the independent, objective, active, and competitive nature which men would bring to nursing could help to accelerate the liberation of these qualities in their female counterparts.[40]

Men are not only perceived as more aggressive, but they are also perceived as more career committed than women. One man said,

I think that men wind up with an advantage in nursing because we can devote all of our time to it. Women usually have other responsibilities. Also, men are more aggressive in the marketplace than women are. Nursing has suffered tremendously because it is a female-dominated profession. And women are just now beginning to come into their own.

Another man noted,

The reason I feel career conditions for nursing are so poor is because from the hospital's standpoint, nurses are terminal employees. They come and go. They have babies. They change careers. For whatever individual reason, they're not there long enough to treat them as permanent employees. . . . Until women as a group treat it as a career and insist upon equal benefits as they have in other careers, it's going to stay as it is.

Later in the interview with this man, it came to light that he had taken several "sabbaticals" from nursing and had switched careers several times. When I asked him if there was a chance he would leave nursing again for an extended period, he said: "I would do it anytime if there was something I thought was worth pursuing. But I wouldn't abandon nursing. I just feel that it's a good backup, and it has allowed me the opportunity to go back to school and do other careers without penalty. I can go back to nursing where I left off essentially." In spite of the fact that his career commitment to nursing was lacking, he blamed women's assumed lack of commitment for the profession's low status.

With this evaluation of the profession in general, it is remarkable that any man would be interested in pursuing nursing in the first place. Indeed, it was not uncommon for male nurses to be critical of men in nursing! One man described his colleagues:

> There are a lot of intelligent men in nursing. And they're all under-achievers as far as I'm concerned for the level of intelligence they possess. Some of the men in the intensive care unit seem brilliant, and they should be doctors, or lawyers, or whatever they want to be. . . . Most of us glide through the nursing program; it's not a great effort. . . . I don't think we're performing to our potential as a group. . . . I think we're taking advantage. We know it's easy, and as long as we do the lifting, do our part, do our nursing duties, we've got a job. So we're not being threatened or pushed. I don't see that as a good quality in us.

Many men I interviewed who did not have high career aspirations were critical of themselves for not being success oriented. They said that nursing was attractive to them because they wanted a job that would not take a lot of work and would provide them with a flexible schedule to enable them to pursue hobbies or other interests. One man said, "In some respects I lead kind of a cavalier lifestyle. . . . I'm irresponsible. I don't want a 9-to-5 job with only two weeks off a year. That's why I work on call." Another man explained one of the reasons nursing originally appealed to him: "I liked the idea that I didn't have to already know what I wanted out of it; that it seemed like a flexible enough field that I could get started and find several paths that I might want to go down. Like I said, I've never been awfully ambitious or real directed."

Men do not enter nursing because they want to defy traditional masculine sex roles. They are attracted to nursing for reasons that have very little to do with gender: It offers extensive employment opportunity and flexible hours, and it requires varying levels of commitment, depending on one's priorities. Many men come to nursing from prior hospital experience, such as orderly or corpsmen work. Aside from the few who said they wanted to be a nurse because they liked the idea of being surrounded by women, the male nurses I interviewed did not seriously deliberate the personal consequences of working in a female-dominated occupation until after they had made the choice. However, once men enter the profession, it becomes very important to them to define their presence as consistent and compatible with a masculine gender identity.

There is a discernible pattern in men's attitudes toward nursing. All agree it is hard, demanding work and that it doesn't warrant its low status. Likewise, they agree that its low status is attributable to its female domination. As men, they have developed two strategies to deal with the problem of lower status: They either pursue administrative or specialized roles in nursing that take them away from primary identification as a low status bedside nurse, or they legitimate their bedside work by referring to their specific personality quirks or character flaws. In the latter case, the men feel compelled to justify their occupational choice as compatible with traditional male gender role activities (ergo, the emphasis on physical strength, different nurturing styles, etc.). In both cases, however, men perceive a conflict between their presence in a female-dominated occupation and the maintenance of their masculinity. They use these various strategies to resolve this tension in a way that unambiguously preserves masculinity intact.

The question of why men do this remains. The answer, I believe, has both an economic (rational) component and an emotional one.

Economically, the various strategies men use to distinguish themselves from female nurses are highly advantageous to them. In the first place, nursing specialties pay higher wages than general ward duty nursing. For example, nurse anesthetists earn on average between $2,248 and $3,112 per month, compared to the average staff nurse salary of approximately $1,500 to $2,000 per month (9.4 percent of all male nurses are anesthetists; 1.1 percent of all registered nurses are anesthetists).[41]

Second, men's and women's assumption that men are more aggressive and possess better leadership abilities enhances male nurses' career mobility. Male nurses are often channeled into the most prestigious and better paying administrative specialties based on this assumption, and they are, for the most part, complicit in this.

Third, the fact that male nurses socialize with physicians more freely than female nurses results in more favorable opportunity for advancement. Floge and Merrill's study found that the informal relationships between male nurses and physicians often result in doctors' positive evaluations and recommendations for their promotion.

And finally, the public's tendency to identify male nurses as physicians heightens the prestige of the men in the eyes of their patients, friends, and families. One nurse told me that he became so weary of explaining to the world that he is a nurse—not a physician—that he eventually gave in and now allows his friends to call him "Doc." Although there are drawbacks to this sort of identification (the discrepancy in salary, for example, could frustrate the physician-identified nurse more intensely than other nurses), it does bring more prestige than if the man were fully accepted as "just a nurse."

This "economic" analysis is convincing: Men's strategies to differentiate their service from that provided by female nurses is wholly consistent with their rational self-interest. Where psychoanalytic theory is helpful is in understanding the particular urgency with which this goal of differentiation is pursued. The men who remain staff nurses are as committed to separating themselves from female nurses as those who specialize or seek administrative career paths. This is due in part to the nature of masculinity: Its viability is predicated on constantly proving that it is better, more "rigorous" somehow, or at least essentially different from femininity. Male nurses have their work cut out for them: Preserving masculinity in an environment so closely associated with femininity is a challenge. No wonder the task is of such central importance in the lives of male nurses.

5

Female Marines and Male Nurses

Most occupations in the U.S. labor force are segregated by sex, but few are more segregated than the nursing profession and the Marine Corps. Approximately half of all U.S. workers are employed in jobs that are at least 80 percent male or female.[1] Female marines and male nurses are truly unusual Americans: They represent less than 5 percent of the work force in their occupations.

Aside from being numerically underrepresented, female marines and male nurses also face similar stereotypes about their chosen fields outside of work. Nurses *are* feminine; marines *are* masculine—anyone will tell you that. The onus is on them to prove otherwise.

One sociological school of thought corroborates this popular view. "Sex role" theory accounts for the differences between men and women in terms of the roles they play in society. Thus, women are "feminine" because they engage in activities, such as mothering, teaching, and nursing, that require them to be emotional, caring, and empathetic. Likewise, men are "masculine" because their roles—family breadwinner, construction worker, soldier—elicit from them such qualities as aggression, discipline, and rationality. Men and women who cross over into nontraditional occupations would thus be expected to assume the gender traits of the opposite sex.

This, of course, is not what happens. This study has examined two groups who have crossed the sex role divide in a most dramatic fashion and yet have *maintained* their gender identity. Female marines are indeed feminine, and male nurses are masculine; gender is maintained even in the most nontraditional occupations.

This is not to suggest, however, that the experiences of women in the military and men in nursing are entirely symmetrical. At work, female marines and male nurses encounter radically different arrangements. Women in the marines face barriers at work that place them at a disadvantage compared to male marines. Official policy bars women from full participation in the Marine Corps, men and women are segregated in basic training, and women are subject to rules intended to maintain their femininity and enhance their essential difference from male marines. But men are welcomed—if not encouraged outright—to enter and practice nursing, they are overrepresented in administrative specialties, and they are treated better than females by physicians. Very little evidence suggests that male nurses as a group encounter any formal or institutionalized discrimination.

Women have been much more eager to join male-dominated occupations than men have been to join female-dominated ones. This is, in part, because of the higher pay and greater status associated with men's jobs. Because of this fact, some have argued that women are excluded from male-dominated occupations because men are "territorial": They perceive women as unwanted competitors for their jobs and construct barriers to them in order to preserve their monopoly over the desirable occupations. Women in female-dominated occupations have the opposite incentive: Many believe that allowing more men in will bring higher salaries and greater social prestige.

There is certainly some truth to this explanation for the asymmetry in the acceptance of women by the Marine Corps and men in nursing. Other studies of women in male-dominated occupations note that greater pay is in fact a major reason women give for entering nontraditional career fields.[2] And the lower status of women's jobs does indeed provide a disincentive for men to join them. Recall, for example, the nurse who said he hoped his own son would choose a profession other than nursing. A daughter who enters a "man's job" has increased her status; a son who does "women's work"—hairdressing, school teaching, or nursing, for example—suffers a decline in status.

However, I have argued throughout this book that, in addition to economic self-interest, there is something even deeper and more fundamental involved in the asymmetry of men's and women's experience in nontraditional occupations: Job segregation by sex allows men to maintain their masculinity in contradistinction to femininity. Men have historically used the occupational realm not only to secure economic advantages over women, but also to establish and affirm their essential difference from—and personal sense of superiority over—women. I have argued, using the psychoanalytic theory of gender identity, that the male psychological need to do this has roots in early childhood experience.

The differences in men's and women's experiences in these two nontraditional occupations ultimately stem from the different perspectives about what it means to be masculine and feminine held by men and women in this society. Men tend to define masculinity negatively—as what is not feminine. For most men raised in this society, "femininity" connotes an inferior state of being relative to masculinity, and the achievement of masculinity is predicated upon superseding whatever is associated with femininity. But feminine gender identity is not something women must prove in contradistinction to masculinity: It is much more consonant with women's self-identity, with the sense of simply *being* female. What one *does* has little or no bearing on feminine gender identity.

Simone de Beauvoir was perhaps the first to describe this asymmetry in gender, which she characterized as a split between "being" and "doing." The young boy's apprenticeship for manhood, she writes, involves "free movement toward the outside world; he contends in hardihood and independence with other boys, he scorns girls. . . . It is by *doing* that he creates his existence."[3] Not so for the little girl, who is taught to conform much more passively to feminine ways. De Beauvoir believed that the "masculine" urge to prove oneself, to demonstrate virility and accomplishment, was clearly superior to the passivity with which girls are taught to approach the world.

Nancy Chodorow picks up on this essential asymmetry but challenges the view that femininity's association with "being" is necessarily inferior to masculinity's focus on "doing." Chodorow argues that women have a much less active concern with affirming their femininity because feminine identity is consonant with their early childhood experiences, whereas masculine identity is not. She believes that all children originally identify with their primary caretakers, their mothers; but because the woman's adult gender identity matches this early identification with her mother, her gender feels as though it has been "ascribed" to her: "She does not need to prove to herself or to society that she has earned it or continues to have it."[4] But unlike girls, boys' achievement of an adult masculine gender identity is predicated on the denial of their earliest (feminine) identifications. Chodorow writes that to achieve masculinity, "a boy represses those qualities he takes to be feminine inside himself, and rejects and devalues women and whatever he considers to be feminine in the social world."[5] As a result of being nurtured exclusively by women as infants, men tend to be more concerned than women with asserting and reaffirming their separateness from members of the opposite sex. Hence, men feel that they must constantly prove to themselves and to others that they are masculine.

The recognition that gender means different things for men and women is a major strength of the psychoanalytic perspective. Understanding the different meanings that men and women attach to gender can help explain its persistence in "nontraditional" occupations. The military is run by men who believe that the achievement of masculinity is a prerequisite for fighting in combat, even though a female marine will tell you that "feminine soldier" is not an oxymoron. Because the military is one arena in which men prove their masculinity, the presence of women—

especially competent women—threatens the achievement of the men's goal to separate and distinguish themselves from women. (Were the military not to have this ideological significance as a "masculinity proving ground," the presence of women would not seem as threatening.) Military policymakers' great pains to preserve military women's femininity (through makeup classes, femininity testing, the combat exclusionary rules, etc.) can thus be seen as veiled attempts to maintain the men's masculinity. If women can do everything men can do, the value of that accomplishment diminishes.

Male nurses also strive to set themselves apart from female nurses. Masculine gender identity is defined as that which is not feminine, so men are more instrumental than women in establishing that difference. Men migrate to the most prestigious and better paying specialties within nursing, thus removing themselves from any association with the "bedside" nurse, or they define their nursing practice in a way that makes it otherwise consistent with masculinity. Some men identify themselves as essentially different in temperament from female nurses: They either describe themselves as more aggressive, independent, and goal oriented than their female colleagues, or they account for their presence in nursing by referring to their character "flaws" (e.g., their lack of commitment to the labor force).

Women do not seem threatened when men enter a predominantly female occupation. Female nurses seem to accept and encourage men in nursing, partly because they believe that men will improve the status of the profession and maybe even increase the salaries. But women are simply not threatened in the same fundamentally psychological way that men are by men's intrusion into a female world of work. Thus, there is a notable absence of restrictions and barriers on men's practice of nursing. (In fact, past barriers emanated largely from other men—particularly military men—who did not want male nurses in the all-female nursing corps.)

There may be sound economic reasons for female nurses to

encourage men to join their ranks. However, the question of why women don't resist the restrictive policies that govern them in the military remains. These policies are, after all, an economic liability for them. Classical psychoanalytic theory accounts for women's apparent complicity with such oppressive institutions by attributing masochistic qualities to the feminine personality: Women consent passively to their subordinate role in society because it gratifies an emotional need for punishment lodged in complex psychological processes. This theory has since been discredited even within the psychoanalytic paradigm, among other reasons because it was originally based on studies of the fantasy lives of *men:* The men Freud studied imagined themselves women in their quest for masochistic gratification.[6] From the point of view of men, it makes sense that only people who enjoy being put down would consent to being labeled feminine. After all, it is a well-known boyhood insult to call another boy a "sissy" or a "girl." To those who disparage femininity, it is impossible to comprehend any positive gratifications associated with feminine-identified activities.

Psychoanalytic theory can shed some light on this question without resorting to the theory of female masochism. My conversations with female marines revealed a deep ambivalence at the core of these women's feminine identification. They indeed want to be thought of as feminine; I have noted that they associate femininity with dignity, bearing, and self-confidence. This I believe is related to women's understanding of femininity as more congruent with qualities typically associated with *humanity*. Yet at the same time, female marines recognize that the majority of male marines do *not* consider femininity an asset.

A paradox therefore arises for women when they are faced with "special treatment" by the men. Should they interpret this behavior as an instance of warranted respect? After all, a feminine woman *does* deserve respect. And, in fact, the new recruits do take the "feminine" drill instructors as role models. Or should this behavior be considered an indication of men's refusal to accept women as full-fledged colleagues in the Marine Corps? As we have seen, this dilemma occasionally expresses itself in a marked ambivalence toward femininity: "Sometimes on the job the men make you a center of attention by wanting to help you. *They think you're incapable or incompetent.* . . . You try not to be rude because sometimes you really do need their help. I think they do that because we're women. *But that's good.* It lets you know that gallantry is not dead." Is it because they think you're incompetent that they treat you this way? Or is it because they want to show you respect and treat you like a "lady"? There is no answer to this question; this paradox reflects a real difference in men's and women's meanings of "femininity." Women consider it an asset; men by and large disparage it. The result is a formidable double bind for women in the marines: They want to be accepted *as women*—and feminine women at that!—in an environment defined by maleness and masculinity and where, by extension, anything associated with being a woman is disparaged.

Female marines have devised various strategies for dealing with this paradox. Some "individualize" the problem. They recognize men's views toward women as derogatory yet see themselves as exceptions to the "rule" of feminine incompetence:

Do you think women should be allowed into combat?

I believe that women cannot handle themselves under that much stress.

How about yourself?

I believe I could handle it. . . . I've always been really good under stress.

This recruit has, to some extent, co-opted men's negative attitude toward femininity, but by taking this contradictory position, she is able to retain her own self-esteem. A similar phenomenon is detected when a woman puts down other women whom she feels are "too" feminine—even though she may pride herself on her own femininity. Both of these positions are efforts to reconcile two unreconcilable views: Men's views toward femininity, which are largely negative, and their own views, which are largely positive.

The other incentive keeping women in the marines from challenging the restrictive policies is that no other option is really viable. As long as men control the military and dominate its organizational hierarchy, women will have no choice but to conform if they wish to remain a part of the Marine Corps. Gender does mean different things to men and women, but because men are in positions of power, their definition and evaluation of the significance of gender is the one that is institutionalized in policy and practice. Men's combined economic *and emotional* self-interests in perpetuating gender differences will ensure their persistence as long as men monopolize the dominant positions in the military.

The study of male nurses and female marines teaches us that occupational integration does not necessarily result in the diminution of gender differences and sexual inequality. In World War II, this was especially evident. Despite their "integration," women in the military and men in nursing were segregated in their duties, and their contributions to the war effort were described in ways entirely compatible with traditional gender qualities. Thus, female marines were offering "support" for the fighting men, even when they replaced full-fledged marines at their duty posts. Male nurses never did get the chance to serve as *nurses* during the war, but those who used their nursing skills in other job classifications were said to be involved in "manly" activities (either because they served on the battlefield or because they tended "masculine" parts of human anatomy, such as genitourinary problems in men). The effects of this "official" integration on the actual sexual segregation of nursing and soldiering were nil: No challenge was ever issued to the "gendered" definitions of nursing as "women's work" and soldiering as "men's work."

Even though there are more women in the Marine Corps and men in nursing today than ever before in history, job segregation continues to persist internally, and the prospects for their future integration remain bleak. Given the "gendered" association of these two occupations, it is unlikely that more women will be allowed into the corps, and it is unlikely that more men will want to become nurses.

Note the asymmetry of the previous statement. I believe that the major reason there are not more women in the Marine Corps is because more are not permitted to join. The new recruits I talked to had joined the Marine Corps for deliberate and rational reasons— not because they yearned to be masculine, not for political or feminist reasons. These women are like the women in blue-collar occupations whom Mary Walshok interviewed and described: "They are not essentially masculine or gay women resolving fundamental gender identity problems through manual labor. They are a complicated, articulate, and interesting group of women with a breadth and depth of experience and insight far beyond what commonsense stereotypes suggest."[7] The military, like most blue-collar male-dominated occupations, holds out the promise for high pay—at least compared to female-dominated civilian occupations.[8] Because from their point of view *money*—not their gender identity—is at stake, I am convinced that many more women would join the Marine Corps if they were actively recruited (as men are) and the arbitrary limits on their participation were lifted.

Other studies on the integration of women into previously "nontraditional" occupations reach the same conclusion. The legal profession, clerical work, and medicine, for example, all previously barred women from entry into practice, either by explicit or unwritten policy. Once these restrictive policies were abandoned, women applied for admission into these fields in overwhelming numbers— despite the popular association each had with being a "male" occupation.[9] As Cohn concludes in his book on the feminization of clerical work in Great Britain, "occupational sex-type is determined largely by the desires of management"—*not* by women's personal trepidations about entering male-defined occupations, nor by their lack of appropriate personality traits needed for these types of jobs.[10] This, of course, corroborates psychoanalytic findings that women are less concerned with maintaining an active compliance with femininity: What one *does* has little or no bearing on how feminine one is. In this regard, the Marine Corps is not unlike any other job—a point constantly reiterated by the female marines I interviewed. One recruit who had left a job in a "doubly eccentric" hair salon to join the Marine Corps told me, "It's like any job you have. . . . I don't think it is any different wearing a uniform in the military and going home and sticking earrings in all four holes in my ears and back to the fuchsia hair colors. You're on your own time when you put your eight hours in." There is no apparent reason why more women wouldn't be equally likely to join the Marine Corps if the opportunity were made available.

Yet, on the contrary, the major reason why there are not more men in nursing is because, in general, men do not want to be nurses—including the men who *are* nurses. Recent efforts to attack the "barriers" to men entering nursing (such as instituting affirmative action policies in nursing schools) are woefully misdirected: It is not discrimination that keeps men out of nursing; it is men's reluctance to enter a "feminine-identified" occupation that keeps them out. Many men I talked to didn't "freely" enter nursing in the first place: They entered the profession from prior hospital experience or because they perceived only limited options available to them. In fact, the men I interviewed told me that nursing was probably the last occupation they would have considered in their youth; its close association as a woman's profession is a formidable barrier to any male otherwise inclined to do this type of work. To encourage more men in nursing, they argued, the first order of business should be to change this feminine connotation. (None of the female marines suggested doing this.) One man even recommended changing the name of the profession because "nursing semantically denotes women—breastfeeding. [It's] considered a female profession, and males in the field [are believed to] have feminine characteristics." As long as nursing is defined as "women's work," men will simply *not want to* engage in it. Not only does nursing pay less than comparable "male" occupations, it has low status by virtue of being female dominated. Not only money, but their higher social status as "masculine" men is at stake when they enter nontraditional occupations.

The heart of the matter is this: The sexual stratification of work reflects men's inability to accept women as equals; it is *not* the result of different personality traits possessed by women and men. The reason men are so extremely underrepresented in nursing is *not* because they lack the necessary "feminine" characteristics required for success in nursing. Nor are there so few women in the Marine Corps because women lack the "masculine" characteristics needed for successful soldiering. In fact, there is nothing "inherently" masculine about the Marine Corps or feminine about nursing. Several of the female marines I interviewed, for example, insisted that the Marine Corps' basic training in discipline and deference is no different from Catholic girls' school education. And in this same vein, a recent history of nursing (based on nurses' memoirs) discovered that "femininity" was more often than not considered a liability by nursing students in the early part of the twentieth century: "As young women converted to the nursing creed, they came to see delicacy and refinement as mere squeamishness, and to view emotional expressiveness as suspect, often a sign of weak and facile sentimentality."[11] My research indicates that most men do not consider becoming a nurse *not* because they're psychologically unsuited for the profession, but rather because they *believe* that nursing is a female occupation that requires the possession of "nonmasculine" character traits—and most men do not want to be considered nonmasculine. Similarly, women have been kept out of the military *not* because they are psychologically unsuited to perform instrumental, nonaffective tasks, but rather because the men in decision-making positions *believe* that women are "too emotional" or that their presence in the military would threaten the "manliness" of the organization. Therefore, in both cases I believe that men control the future of integration.

This rather pessimistic conclusion does not bode well for an end to occupational sex segregration. The roots of this social organization are lodged deeply and securely in our current system of gender identity formation. As long as men feel a psychological need to separate and distinguish themselves from women—as long as their own adult gender identity is premised upon denying and denigrating whatever they conceive to be feminine—they will continue to desire that certain activities remain "for men only."

At the very least, this means that female-dominated occupations have little prospect of attracting men to them as long as they remain "feminine identified." This seems to be borne out by historical studies of occupations. Those occupations that changed from female dominated to male dominated—medicine, for example—effectively challenged that feminine identification prior to the entrance of large numbers of men into practice. The work itself was redefined and in the process made into a legitimate activity for "masculine" men (which, of course, entailed discrediting the contemporary female practitioners and excluding women from the "new" profession of medicine).[12] Similarly, countries that have larger percentages of men in the nursing profession, such as Australia, do so only because the highly technical areas in which male nurses work have been successfully demarcated and distinguished from the caring, nurturing work of the "feminine" nurse.[13]

However, men's ability to continue to segregate "male only" activities depends upon their continuing to monopolize the most powerful, policy-making positions in the male-dominated organizations. If women could themselves enter such powerful positions, the possibility for transforming them might present itself. Affirmative action policies and antidiscrimination legislation hold out precisely this promise for change. Studies have found that these policies are indeed effective in reducing occupational sex stratification—particularly in blue-collar occupations where resistance to women is often more explicit and organized.[14] Deaux and Ullman, for example, conclude in their study of women in the steel industry that affirmative action "policy was an effective one, contributing to sharp rises in female employment in the industry.

An energetic and committed implementation of equal opportunity and affirmative action programs can have positive employment effects for the target groups without serious harm to the employers."[15]

However, forcing men to accept women into "their" occupations will not eliminate the foundation upon which sexual stratification is based. The final solution to occupational segregation would entail an even more profound social reorganization. Only if our child-rearing arrangements change so that women are no longer solely responsible for the care of infants in our society—so that the attainment of masculinity no longer requires separation from a primary feminine identification—only then would there be a real challenge to the psychological desires at the root of sexual segregation. There may indeed be some truth to Major Gabriel's comment on the integration of the army: "An aspect bearing directly upon the ability of military groups to integrate females is that it is likely to require among the male members their complete redefinition of themselves as 'men.' "[16] Likewise, an understanding of what is at stake in integration can be gained from this comment by a male nurse in the air force: "Not all men are cut out to be nurses. If a man's identity is threatened, he will not feel secure in a nursing position." The achievement of masculinity is today intertwined with demonstrating superiority and essential difference from females. It is this meaning of masculinity—deeply rooted as it is in personality and, ultimately, family structure—that must be challenged if any real inroads toward sexual integration and, ultimately, sexual equality can be attained.

Methodological Appendix

Data for this project were gathered from a variety of sources using different research techniques. The main source of information is formal, in-depth interviews I conducted with women in the military and men in nursing in various locations throughout the United States.

Here is the "breakdown" of the individuals I interviewed in the military:

1. Six officers (three male and three female) stationed in the San Francisco Bay Area, in their offices, 1984
2. Six air force officers (two male, four female) stationed at a southwestern air force base, in their offices, 1985
3. Six Pentagon officials, in their offices in Washington, D.C., 1984
4. Ten World War II female marine veterans at the convention site of the Women Marines Association, 1984
5. Twenty-one female marine recruits, fourteen female marine drill instructors, three female marine officers, one male marine sergeant, all interviewed at Parris Island, South Carolina, 1985

The interviews conducted at Parris Island were tape-recorded (in all but two cases), and I transcribed them for analysis. I made no effort to select my respondents randomly or systematically.

Rather, I requested interviews with women from a wide variety of backgrounds and with varying levels of commitment to the Marine Corps. I was granted complete freedom of access to interview whomever I wanted. I was also given a private office in which to conduct interviews.

I was sensitive to the fact that the women recruits I chose to interview were not free to refuse to be interviewed. (They are under strict orders to obey all commands issued by their drill instructors. In a sense, they were "commanded" to subject themselves to be interviewed.) I presented each with a consent form and carefully went over it with her before starting the interview. Some version of this form was given to all people who agreed to be interviewed for this project. In no case did the individual decline to be interviewed, however. I perceived in all cases that the recruits viewed the opportunity to talk and relax with a civilian a welcomed break from the vigorous regime of basic training.

As two additional sources of interview data, I administered written surveys to a group of 12 female ROTC naval cadets (6 were returned) and to the 200 participants in the Women Marines Association convention (46 were returned).

I also took extensive field notes while observing and participating in various aspects of basic training. During the two weeks I spent on Parris Island, I became quite familiar with certain drill instructors who welcomed me into their offices to chat while I was awaiting scheduled interviews. These unstructured, informal discussions provided me with incredibly rich insights into women's experiences in the Marine Corps.

I conducted a total of twenty-one formal, in-depth interviews with men in nursing for this project. Here is the "breakdown" of those I interviewed (all in 1985):

1. Six nursing students
2. Three professors of nursing in baccalaureate programs
3. Twelve practicing registered nurses
4. Five practicing female registered nurses

Most of the interviews with male nurses were conducted in the San Francisco Bay Area. They took place at my office, in restaurants, in coffee shops, and in some cases in the nurse's home. I was fortunate to be invited to the annual convention of the American Assembly for Men in Nursing (AAMN) on two occasions, in 1985 and again in 1986. I conducted several interviews at the convention site. Most of my convention respondents were from the Midwest and the eastern part of the United States. All but two interviews with male nurses were tape-recorded, and I transcribed them for analysis.

I administered a written survey to participants of the 1985 AAMN convention. I received 27 returns out of approximately 100 distributed.

I also had more informal sources of data to study male nurses. At the AAMN conventions, I again took extensive field notes and participated in numerous informal discussions. I also had the opportunity to observe a discussion session on men in nursing as a minority, attended by fifteen male nurses, which turned out to be an incredibly rich source of information. I was subsequently invited to present my research to a local San Francisco chapter of the AAMN. I gained further insight into many issues from the thoughtful comments of those who attended my presentation.

Concerning interviewing difficulties posed by being female, I suspect that my sex did influence how the men I interviewed responded to my questions. After all, in the course of the interviews, many men asserted very firm beliefs about the existence of fundamental differences between the sexes (regarding, for example, emotional disposition, professional interests, and inherent capabilities). I do not believe that people were actually dishonest with me because I am female. However, some may have been reluctant to be completely candid about their feelings toward female nurses, for example, perceiving that I might disapprove of those feelings because I am female.[1] This problem is ultimately insurmountable. The most one can do in this situation is to pay close and sensitive attention to the details of personal interviewing style. For this reason, I believe that male researchers who use interviewing methods could make essential contributions to the study of men in nontraditional occupations. I am unaware of any men currently engaged in this type of research; yet I believe the need is definitely there.

In what follows I reproduce in schematic form the basic schedule I used for conducting in-depth interviews. However, the interviews did not necessarily follow this order, and additional questions were always asked to probe general responses. Interviews lasted between forty-five minutes and two and a half hours, with most taking approximately one to one and a half hours. The interviews with nurses typically lasted twice as long as those with individuals in the military, probably due to the more informal contexts in which they took place.

INTERVIEW SCHEDULE

I. Background Questions

When did you first decide to become a marine/nurse?

Had you ever thought of joining this occupation before then?

Is anyone in your family a marine/nurse? Did you discuss joining with him/her?

What was your image of the Marine Corps/nursing profession before you joined it? What did you consider to be the positive features of the Marine Corps/nursing profession? The drawbacks?

Describe to me how you came to decide to join. What was going on in your life at the time? What were your options?

Marines: Why did you choose this branch of the service and not the navy or air force or army?

Nurses: Did you ever consider becoming a physician?

Did you have any role models that you sought to emulate?

What were the reactions of your friends/family to your decision to become a marine/nurse?

Did you have any hesitation about joining because of your sex?

II. Training Experience

Describe to me your training experience.

Do you have a specialization? How did you come to select this particular one?

In basic training/nursing school, do you think you were treated any differently on account of your sex? Were you excluded from any aspect of training?

Is there any part of your training that you would like to see changed? What aspects ought to be maintained?

Do you think that there is a particular type of woman/man who is most likely to succeed in basic training/nursing school? Is there a particular type of woman/man who is unlikely to succeed?

Nurses: How many men were in your graduating class? Did you socialize more frequently with them than your female peers?

III. On-the-Job Experience

Describe your employment history. Where do you work now? Where would you like to work in the future?

How many other women/men work with you at your present job? How well do they accept you? Have you ever encountered discrimination from your peers where you worked because of your sex? From your superiors/supervisors and physicians? Do you know anyone who has experienced such discrimination?

Do you think women in the Marine Corps/men in nursing bring special qualities to their occupations? Do you think Women Marines/male nurses are suited to a particular role in the Marine Corps/nursing profession?

Where do you see yourself in ten years?

Marines: What do you think about the combat exclusionary

rules in the military? Would you like the chance to serve in combat? What do you think about the higher entrance standards required of female recruits? The makeup and poise classes?

IV. General Issues

What do you think would have to happen for there to be more women in the Marine Corps/men in nursing? Are these things likely to happen?

If you had it to do all over again, would you enter the Marine Corps/nursing profession?

Are you married? Do you have children? Do you expect to marry and have children? If you had a daughter/son, would you encourage her/him to enter the Marine Corps/ nursing profession?

What are the benefits of being a woman in the Marine Corps/man in nursing? What are the drawbacks?

Notes

I INTRODUCTION

1. Advertisement reprinted in Beatrice J. Kalisch and Philip A. Kalisch, *Politics of Nursing* (Philadelphia: J. B. Lippincott, 1982), p. 175.

2. These 1981 percentages are all from Andrea Beller and Kee-Ok Kim Han, "Occupational Sex Segregation: Prospects for the 1980s," in *Sex Segregation in the Workplace: Trends, Explanations, Remedies,* ed. Barbara Reskin (Washington, D.C.: National Academy Press, 1984), pp. 106–11.

3. Barbara F. Reskin and Heidi I. Hartmann, *Women's Work, Men's Work: Sex Segregation on the Job* (Washington, D.C.: National Academy Press, 1986), p. 7.

4. "Woman Marine" is the official title used to designate all women in the Marine Corps. It is typically capitalized in their publications. There is no equivalent term for men; they are simply called "marines" or, in some cases, "male marines"—not capitalized. Likewise, men in nursing have no "official" title.

Some linguists have argued that the term "male nurse" is demeaning and sexist because it implies that *real* nurses are always female. See Casey Miller and Kate Swift, *The Handbook of Nonsexist Writing* (New York: Lippincott & Crowell, 1980), pp. 55–56.

Certainly when the modifier is used gratuitously, this conclusion is warranted. One nurse I interviewed, for example, was disgusted by many who asked him, "How do you like male nursing?"— implying that what he did was somehow not really nursing. I have made every effort to avoid such gratuitous usage and to use the modifiers "male" and "female" only when discussing meaningful and significant differences.

5. William Bielby and James N. Baron, "A Woman's Place Is with Other Women: Sex Segregation Within Organizations," in Reskin, *Sex Segregation,* pp. 27–55.

6. Barbara Reskin and Patricia Roos, "Status Hierarchies and Sex Segregation," in *Ingredients for Women's Employment Policy,* ed. Christine Bose and Glenna Spitze (Albany: State University of New York Press, 1987), p. 12.

7. U.S. Department of Defense, Manpower Installations and Logistics, *Military Women in the Department of Defense* (Washington, D.C.: Government Printing Office, 1984), p. v.

8. Reskin and Roos, "Status Hierarchies," p. 17.

9. Rosabeth Moss Kanter, *Men and Women of the Corporation* (New York: Basic Books, 1977).

10. Kanter, *Men and Women,* pp. 213–15.

11. Quoted in Jeanne Holm, *Women in the Military: An Unfinished Revolution* (Novato, Calif.: Presidio Press, 1982), p. 278.

12. Sigmund Freud, "The Dissection of the Psychical Personality," in *New Introductory Lectures on Psychoanalysis* (1933; New York: Norton, 1965), p. 52.

13. Robert Stoller, *Sex and Gender: On the Development of Masculinity and Femininity* (New York: Science House, 1968); Harold Garfinkel, "Passing and the Managed Achievement of Sex Status in an Intersexed Person, Part I," in *Studies in Ethnomethodology* (Englewood Cliffs, N.J.: Prentice-Hall, 1967), pp. 116–85. For a more recent example of gender scholarship on transsexuals, see Suzanne Kessler and Wendy McKenna, *Gender: An Ethnomethodological Approach* (New York: Wiley, 1978).

14. Heidi Hartmann made this argument in "The Unhappy

Marriage of Marxism and Feminism," *Capital and Class* 8 (1979): 1–33: "Even when men and women do not actually behave in the way sexual norms prescribe, men *claim for themselves* those characteristics which are valued in the dominant ideology" (p. 21, emphasis in original).

15. Heidi Hartmann, "The Family as Locus of Gender, Class, and Political Struggle: The Example of Housework," *Signs* 6:3 (Spring 1981): 372.

16. Child rearing is sometimes cited as an undesirable task left to women because men do not want to do it. Margaret Polatnick, "Why Men Don't Rear Children: A Power Analysis," *Berkeley Journal of Sociology* 18 (1974): 45–86, writes: "Whatever the 'intrinsic desirability' of rearing children, the conditions of the job as it's now constituted—no salary, low status, long hours, domestic isolation—mark it as a job for women only. Men, as the superordinate group, don't want child-rearing responsibility, so they assign it to women. Women's functioning as child-rearers reinforces, in turn, their subordinate position" (p. 79).

17. Quoted in Michael Wright, "The Marine Corps Faces the Future," *New York Times Magazine,* June 20, 1982, p. 74.

18. Jean Lipman-Bluman, *Gender Roles and Power* (Englewood Cliffs, N.J.: Prentice-Hall, 1984), p. 59.

19. For a review of the history of sex role theory, see Tim Carrigan, Bob Connell, and John Lee, "Toward a New Sociology of Masculinity," *Theory and Society* 14 (September 1985): 551–603.

20. Talcott Parsons and Robert Bales, *Family: Socialization and Interaction Process* (Glencoe, Ill.: Free Press, 1955).

21. Although Parsons uses psychoanalysis in his theory of personality formation, the dynamic interaction between the individual and the forces of socialization is distinctly absent. Parsons argues that even the id is the *product* of social organization. See "The Superego and the Theory of Social Systems," in *Social Structure and Personality* (1952; New York: Free Press, 1970). The result is a model of individual personality development completely determined by socializing agencies. As D. H. J. Morgan notes, Par-

sons's writings on the subject "at best show a strong unilateral bias and at worst betray an astonishing lack of sensitivity to human creativity and variability." See his *Social Theory and the Family* (London: Routledge and Kegan Paul, 1975), p. 41.

22. Nancy Chodorow, *The Reproduction of Mothering* (Berkeley and Los Angeles: University of California Press, 1978).

23. Chodorow, *The Reproduction*, p. 174.

24. Robert Stoller, *Presentations of Gender* (New Haven, Conn.: Yale University Press, 1985), p. 18.

25. Stoller, *Presentations*, p 17.

2 INTEGRATING THE MARINE CORPS AND NURSING

1. Prior to 1973 there was a 2 percent cap on female enlistments. As a result in 1972, for example, only 1.6 percent of all military personnel were female. U.S. Department of Defense, Office of the Assistant Secretary of Defense (Manpower, Reserve Affairs and Logistics), *Uses of Women in the Military*, 2d ed., 1978.

2. Jeanne Holm, *Women in the Military: An Unfinished Revolution* (Novato, Calif.: Presidio Press, 1982), p. 108.

3. Holm, *Women in the Military*, p. 107.

4. Susan M. Hartmann, *The Home Front and Beyond: American Women in the 1940's* (Boston: Twayne, 1982), p. 43.

5. Mattie E. Treadwell, *The Women's Army Corps* (Washington, D.C.: U.S. Army Office of Military History, 1954), p. 403.

6. D'Ann Campbell, *Women at War with America* (Cambridge, Mass.: Harvard University Press, 1984), p. 27.

7. Service women discharged for pregnancy had to pay their own maternity expenses; servicemen's wives were given free medical care.

8. Treadwell, *The Women's Army Corps*, p. 590.

9. Treadwell, *The Women's Army Corps*, pp. 597–98.

10. Jack D. Foner, *Blacks and the Military in American History* (New York: Praeger, 1974), p. 174.

11. Ruth Milkman, *Gender at Work: The Dynamics of Job Segregation by Sex During World War II* (Urbana: University of Illinois Press, 1987), pp. 49–50.

12. Treadwell, *The Women's Army Corps,* p. 19.

13. Treadwell, *The Women's Army Corps,* p. 19.

14. Regulations cited in Holm, *Women in the Military,* pp. 62–63.

15. Treadwell, *The Women's Army Corps,* p. 301.

16. Treadwell, *The Women's Army Corps,* p. 302.

17. Campbell, *Women at War,* p. 39.

18. Susan M. Hartmann, "Women in the Military Service," in *Clio Was a Woman,* ed. M. E. Deutrich and V. C. Purdy (Washington, D.C.: Howard University Press, 1980), p. 195.

19. Campbell, *Women at War,* p. 36.

20. Male and female units typically dined in separate facilities and had different "master menus" or standard dietary fare. Women, who demanded less heavy and fattening foods, were typically served meals with more fresh vegetables and salads. Treadwell, *The Women's Army Corps,* discusses these mess modifications in the army on pp. 526–27.

21. The army and the navy officially denied all reports of homosexuality. The Marine Corps, however, used psychiatric tests as well as overt evidence ultimately to dismiss twenty women (out of twenty-three thousand) for lesbianism. See Campbell, *Women at War,* p. 28.

22. Treadwell, *The Women's Army Corps,* p. 206.

23. Michael Rustad, *Women in Khaki: The American Enlisted Woman* (New York: Praeger, 1982), p. 29.

24. Treadwell, *The Women's Army Corps,* p. 738.

25. Treadwell, *The Women's Army Corps,* p. 739.

26. Campbell, *Women at War,* p. 45.

27. These problems are still in evidence today. See "Sex Bias Is Found at V.A. Hospitals," *New York Times,* September 30, 1982, p. CII.

28. Campbell, *Women at War,* p. 53.

29. Philip A. Kalisch and Beatrice J. Kalisch, *The Advance of American Nursing* (Boston: Little, Brown, 1978), p. 480.

30. Kalisch and Kalisch, *The Advance,* p. 453.

31. Regulations cited in the U.S. Congressional Record (Washington, D.C.: Government Printing Office, 1945), p. 1725.

32. Campbell, *Women at War,* p. 53.

33. U.S. Congressional Record, p. 1739.

34. The most infamous example is that of the navy nurses present at the fall of Bataan and Corregidor who were forced into extremely dangerous and wretched conditions; several were taken prisoner of war. For an account of their experiences, see Kalisch and Kalisch, *The Advance,* p. 476.

35. Edward L. Bernays, "The Armed Services and the Nursing Profession," *American Journal of Nursing* 46 (1946): 166.

36. Quoted in Kalisch and Kalisch, *The Advance,* p. 457.

37. Campbell, *Women at War,* pp. 57–58.

38. In March 1945, the first black nurse entered the Navy Nurse Corps, only a few months prior to the end of the war. Altogether, four black nurses were on active duty during World War II in the Navy Nurse Corps. See Mary Elizabeth Carnegie, *The Path We Tread: Blacks in Nursing, 1854–1984* (Philadelphia: Lippincott, 1986), p. 177.

39. Darlene Clark Hine, "Mabel K. Staupers and the Integration of Black Nurses into the Armed Forces," in *Black Leaders of the Twentieth Century,* ed. J. H. Franklin and A. Meier (Urbana: University of Illinois Press, 1982), p. 248.

40. There were very few black male nurses at the start of World War II. In 1940, there were only 127 black male graduate *and* student nurses. The combination of racial and sexual stratification of nursing schools made nursing education for black men virtually nonexistent. Twenty-one states were reported as having no black male nurses or students in 1940. See Estelle Massey Osborne, "Status and Contribution of the Negro Nurse," *Journal of Negro Education* 18 (1949): 367.

41. Quoted in the appendix to the U.S. Congressional Record (Washington, D.C.: Government Printing Office, February 26, 1945), p. A838.

42. *American Journal of Nursing* 44 (1944): 519.

43. Men were allowed into the Cadet Nursing Corps, but their studies did not qualify them for deferments. Thus, in 1944 there were only seventeen male nursing students in the CNC.

44. *American Journal of Nursing* 44 (1944): 770–71. Emphasis added.

45. Appendix to the U.S. Congressional Record, February 26, 1945, p. A838.

46. *American Journal of Nursing* 44 (1944): 519.

47. *American Journal of Nursing* 44 (1944): 909.

48. *American Journal of Nursing* 45 (1945): 960.

49. *American Journal of Nursing* 44 (1944): 771.

50. Quoted in the appendix to the U.S. Congressional Record, February 26, 1945, p. A838.

51. Mr. Somers, U.S. Representative from New York, during the debate on the House floor to approve the establishment of the WAAC, in the U.S. Congressional Record, March 17, 1942, p. 2606.

3   FEMININITY IN THE MARINE CORPS

1. Quoted in Robert L. Nabors, "Women in the Army: Do They Measure Up?" *Military Review* 62:10 (October 1982): 52.

2. Women's Equity Action League, *WEAL Facts,* 1984, p. 4.

3. *San Francisco Chronicle,* January 18, 1985, p. 17.

4. U.S. Department of Defense, Office of the Assistant Secretary of Defense (Manpower, Reserve Affairs, and Logistics), *Use of Women in the Military,* 2d ed., September 1978, p. 2.

5. Jeanne Holm, *Women in the Military: An Unfinished Revolution* (Novato, Calif.: Presidio Press, 1982), pp. 256–57.

6. Quoted in U.S. Department of Defense, Office of the Assistant Secretary of Defense, *Use of Women,* p. 2.

7. U.S. Army Research Institute, *Women Content in Units*

Force Development Test (*MAXWAC*), 1977, foreword. Category II and III refer to combat support and combat service support units, respectively.

8. U.S. Army Research Institute, *Women Content,* p. I-3.

9. Martin Binkin and Shirley J. Bach, *Women and the Military* (Washington, D.C.: Brookings Institution, 1977).

10. Georgia Clark Sadler, "Women in the Sea Services: 1972–1982," *U.S. Naval Institute Proceedings* (1983): 147.

11. Kathleen Jones, "Dividing the Ranks: Women and the Draft," *Women & Politics* 4:4 (Winter 1985): 77.

12. Jeff M. Tuten, "The Argument Against Female Combatants," in *Female Soldiers—Combatants or Noncombatants?* ed. Nancy L. Goldman (Westport, Conn.: Greenwood Press, 1982), p. 248.

13. Daniel Rapoport, "Women in Combat," *National Journal,* July 17, 1982, p. 1266. Also see the excellent discussion of the women in combat issue in Jane J. Mansbridge, *Why We Lost the ERA* (Chicago: University of Chicago Press, 1986), esp. pp. 60–89.

14. Richard A. Gabriel, "Women in Combat?" *Army,* March 1980, p. 49.

15. Mady Segal, "The Argument for Female Combatants," in Goldman, *Female Soldiers,* p. 268.

16. Mady Segal, "Women's Roles in the U.S. Armed Forces: An Evaluation of Evidence and Arguments for Policy Decisions," in *Conscripts and Volunteers* ed. Robert K. Fullinwider (Totowa, N.J.: Rowman and Allenheld, 1983), p. 202.

17. Judith Hicks Stiehm, "The Protected, the Protector, the Defender," *Women's Studies International Forum* 5:3/4 (1982): 367–76.

18. Quoted in Holm, *Women in the Military,* p. 338.

19. This is precisely what happened during the U.S. invasion of Grenada in 1983. Several female pilots, flight engineers, and load masters flew missions into Grenada and were exposed to combat fire. According to air force sources contacted by the *Los Angeles Times,* women were used because "invasion planning was

so swift . . . that there was no time to handpick the crews of airlift aircraft." *Los Angeles Times,* January 26, 1986, p. 6.

20. Quoted in Holm, *Women in the Military,* p. 341.

21. *Navy Times,* September 13, 1982, p. 7.

22. Quoted in Holm, *Women in the Military,* p. 383.

23. *Army Times,* September 6, 1982, p. 10.

24. Quoted in Holm, *Women in the Military,* p. 384.

25. Cynthia Enloe, *Does Khaki Become You?* (London: Pluto Press, 1983), p. 158; Michael Rustad, *Women in Khaki* (New York: Praeger, 1982), p. 64.

26. Pete Earley, "Women Ask If Army Is Going Off Limits," *Washington Post,* August 4, 1982, p. 17; personal communication at the Pentagon, October 1984.

27. *Baltimore Sun,* May 4, 1982, p. 3.

28. "Bob Levy's Washington," WRC radio, Washington, D.C., October 19, 1982.

29. *Washington Post,* August 4, 1982, p. 17.

30. Personal communication at the Pentagon, October 1984.

31. U.S. Department of the Army, Office of the Deputy Chief of Staff for Personnel, *Women in the Army Policy Review,* 1982, p. 10.

32. U.S. Department of the Army, Office of the Deputy Chief of Staff for Personnel, *Women in the Army,* pp. 4–9.

33. *Army Times,* September 13, 1982, p. 3.

34. *Washington Post,* August 27, 1982, p. 1.

35. *Los Angeles Times,* August 27, 1982, p. 12.

36. *New York Times,* September 9, 1982.

37. Elyse W. Kerce and Marjorie H. Royle, *First-Term Enlisted Marine Corps Women: Their Backgrounds and Experiences* (San Diego, Calif.: Navy Personnel Research and Development Center, 1984), p. 16.

38. John C. Woelfel, "Women in the United States Army," *Sex Roles* 7 (1981): 796; emphasis added.

39. B. G. Beck, "Women as Warriors: A Study in Contrasts," *Army,* February 1981, p. 30.

40. Sadler, "Women in the Sea Services," p. 145; emphasis added.

41. Gabriel, "Women in Combat?" p. 50.

42. *Los Angeles Times,* August 29, 1985, p. 11.

43. U.S. Marine Corps, Marine Corps Institute, *The United States Marine—Essential Subjects,* 1983, foreword.

44. U.S. Marine Corps, Marine Corps Institute, *The United States Marine,* pp. 6–35.

45. Poise and etiquette classes include instruction on proper behavior in public. Women recruits are taught the correct way to walk (always in step with good posture), how to sit, and how to smoke properly.

46. Judith Hicks Stiehm, *Bring Me Men and Women: Mandated Change at the U.S. Air Force Academy* (Berkeley and Los Angeles: University of California Press, 1981), p. 253.

47. Gabriel, "Women in Combat?" p. 50.

48. Lillian Rubin, *Intimate Strangers* (New York: Harper and Row, 1983), pp. 42–43.

49. Robert Stoller, *Presentations of Gender* (New Haven, Conn.: Yale University Press, 1985), p. 17.

50. Sigmund Freud, "Some Psychological Consequences of the Anatomical Distinction Between the Sexes," in *Sexuality and the Psychology of Love* (1925; New York: Collier Books, 1963), p. 187.

51. Rosabeth Moss Kanter, "Some Effects of Proportions on Group Life: Skewed Sex Ratios and Responses to Token Women," *American Journal of Sociology* 82 (March 1977): 975.

52. Kerce and Royle, *First-Term Enlisted,* p. 16.

53. U.S. Department of Defense, Office of the Assistant Secretary of Defense (Manpower, Reserve Affairs, and Logistics), *Profile of American Youth* (Washington, D.C.: Government Printing Office, 1982), p. 23.

54. U.S. Department of Defense (Manpower, Installations and Logistics), *Military Women in the Department of Defense,* 1984, p. 49.

55. Jack Hicks, "Women in the Army," *Armed Forces and Society* 4:4 (August 1978): 650.

56. Binkin and Bach, *Women and the Military,* p. 32.

57. Kerce and Royle, *First-Term Enlisted,* p. 7.

58. Women in the marines constantly criticize women in the army for not maintaining their femininity. I had asked this recruit to compare women in the two branches because she had worked as a civilian in an army office before she enlisted in the marines, and we had discussed her experience there earlier in the interview.

59. Kerce and Royle, *First-Term Enlisted,* p. 7.

60. One of the two who was not willing to go into combat cited religious reasons for her opposition to fighting in general. The other would refuse because she said it was understood that she wouldn't have to when she joined (i.e., she felt she had a contractual agreement with the military not to have to fight).

4   MASCULINITY IN NURSING

1. Elizabeth Jamieson, Mary Sewall, and Lucille S. Gjertson, *Trends in Nursing History* (Philadelphia: Saunders, 1959), p. 477.

2. American Nurses' Association, *Facts About Nursing* (Kansas City, Mo.: American Nurses' Association, 1950), p. 46.

3. Mary Roberts, *American Nursing: History and Interpretation* (New York: Macmillan, 1954), p. 313.

4. Josephine Dolan, *Nursing in Society* (Philadelphia: Saunders, 1978), p. 308.

5. Roberts, *American Nursing,* p. 322.

6. Roberts, *American Nursing,* p. 324.

7. American Nurses' Association, *Facts About Nursing,* p. 46.

8. Roberts, *American Nursing,* p. 323.

9. Roberts, *American Nursing,* p. 322.

10. U.S. House of Representatives, Committee on Armed Services, Subcommittee No. 2, *Subcommittee Hearings on H.R. 2559* (July 7, 1955), p. 4290.

11. U.S. House of Representatives, *Subcommittee Hearings,* p. 4293.

12. U.S. House of Representatives, *Subcommittee Hearings,* p. 4293.

13. U.S. House of Representatives, *Subcommittee Hearings,* p. 4296.

14. Recall, however, that those female nurses who did serve in combat zones in World War II were awarded high military honors for their valor and superior performance.

15. *Regan Report on Nursing Law* 23:5 (October 1982): 1.

16. Janet Gans, "Sex Differences in Tokens' Career Attainment," paper presented at the 1983 annual meeting of the Society for the Study of Social Problems, Detroit, Michigan, 1983, p. 7; Emily Greenberg and Burton Levine, "Role Strain in Men Nurses," *Nursing Forum* 10:4 (1971): 416–30.

17. *Regan Report on Nursing Law,* p. 4.

18. *Time Magazine* 120:2 (July 12, 1982): 23.

19. Janet Gans, "The Mobile Minority: Men's Success in a Woman's Profession," Ph.D. dissertation, University of Massachusetts, May 1984, p. 56.

20. Gans, "The Mobile Minority," pp. 64–65.

21. Heidi Hartmann, "The Family as Locus of Gender, Class, and Political Struggle: The Example of Housework," *Signs* 6:3 (Spring 1981): 366–94.

22. Rosabeth Moss Kanter, *Men and Women of the Corporation* (New York: Basic Books, 1977).

23. Gans, "The Mobile Minority," p. 94.

24. James McCarragher, "Attitudes of Nurses Toward the Male Nurse: A Question of Stigma," master's thesis, Case Western Reserve University, School of Nursing, 1984, p. 52.

25. Myron D. Fottler, "Attitudes of Female Nurses Toward the Male Nurse: A Study of Occupational Segregation," *Journal of Health and Social Behavior* 17 (June 1976): 99–111.

26. Liliane Floge and Deborah M. Merrill, "Tokenism Reconsidered: Male Nurses and Female Physicians in a Hospital Setting," paper presented at the 80th meeting of the American Sociological Association, Washington, D.C., August 28, 1985, p. 8.

27. *Regan Report on Nursing Law,* p. 1.

28. Gans, "The Mobile Minority."

29. Floge and Merrill, "Tokenism Reconsidered."

30. Barbara J. Holtzclaw, "The Man in Nursing: Relationship Between Sex-Typed Perceptions and Locus of Control," Ph.D. dissertation, University of Oklahoma, School of Nursing, 1984; Bonnie J. Garvin, "Values of Male Nursing Students," *Nursing Research* 25:5 (September 1976): 352–57; Jean C. Aldag and Cherryl Christensen, "Personality Correlates of Male Nurses," *Nursing Research* 16 (1967): 375–76.

31. Sandy F. Mannino, "The Professional Man Nurse: Why He Chose Nursing and Other Characteristics of Men in Nursing," *Nursing Research* 12:3 (Summer 1963): 185–87.

32. Garvin, "Values," p. 356.

33. Ronald G. S. Brown and Robert W. H. Stones, *The Male Nurse* (London: G. Bell & Sons, 1973); Mannino, "The Professional"; Garvin, "Values."

34. Adrian Schoenmaker, "Nursing's Dilemma: Male vs. Female Admissions Choice," *Nursing Forum* 15 (1976): 406–12; Brown and Stones, *The Male Nurse;* Mannino, "The Professional."

35. Dolores Vaz, "High School Senior Boys' Attitudes Towards Nursing as a Career," *Nursing Research* 17:6 (November–December 1968): 533–38.

36. Floge and Merrill, "Tokenism Reconsidered."

37. I asked one nurse from the Midwest whether he thought nurses from the San Francisco Bay Area are in any way "different" from nurses in the Midwest. He responded, "Oh, yes, they're all fruits out there!"

38. Statistics gathered by the American Nurses' Association indicate that 23.7 percent of female nurses are not employed in nursing, as compared to 13.8 percent of all male nurses (American Nurses' Association, *Facts About Nursing, 84–85* [Kansas City, Mo.: American Nurses' Association, 1985], pp. 23–24). These data were not analyzed to show what portion of these nurses were employed in other fields. One study reports that only 3 percent of

all nurses are employed in fields other than nursing (P. McCarty, "Survey Shows a Million RN's Are Employed," *American Nurse* 12:9 [1980], pp. 1, 6, 10). It is conceivable that a greater proportion of the male nurses who are not employed in nursing are employed in other fields (as compared to female nurses), but this information is not available.

39. This percentage was probably based on a 1971 national survey of 220 nurses that found that within two years of beginning practice, about half the sample exited from hospital practice. Approximately one-third of the sample left nursing altogether (Marlene Kramer and Constance Baker, "The Exodus: Can We Prevent It?" *Journal of Nursing Administration* 1 [1971]: 15–30). The American Nurses' Association estimates that 76 percent of all registered nurses in 1980 were employed in nursing (*Facts About Nursing, 84–85:* 22). This represents one of the highest labor force participation rates of any female-dominated occupation in the United States (Linda H. Aiken, Roger Blendon, and David Rogers, "The Shortage of Hospital Nurses: A New Perspective," in *Nursing Issues and Nursing Strategies for the Eighties,* ed. Bonnie Bullough, Vern Bullough, and Mary Soukup [New York: Springer, 1983], p. 25).

40. Michael Beebe, Steve Barr and Mary Hamilton, "Anatomy Is Destiny," in Bullough, *Nursing Issues,* p. 42.

41. American Nurses' Association, *Facts About Nursing,* 1985, pp. 25–26, 170, 172.

5   FEMALE MARINES AND MALE NURSES

1. Barbara Reskin and Heidi Hartmann, *Women's Work, Men's Work: Sex Segregation on the Job* (Washington, D.C.: National Academy Press, 1986), p. 7.

2. Two recent studies of women in blue-collar occupations make this point using in-depth interview data. They are Jean Reith Schroedel, *Alone in a Crowd: Women in the Trades Tell Their Stories* (Philadelphia: Temple University Press, 1985), and Mary Lindenstein Walshok, *Blue-Collar Women: Pioneers on the Male Frontier* (Garden City, N.Y.: Anchor Press, 1981). See also Kay

Deaux and Joseph Ullman, *Women of Steel* (New York: Praeger, 1983), esp. p. 33.

3. Simone de Beauvoir, *The Second Sex* (New York: Knopf, 1957), p. 280.

4. Nancy Chodorow, "Being and Doing: A Cross-Cultural Examination of the Socialization of Males and Females," in *Women in Sexist Society,* ed. Vivian Gornick and Barbara Moran (New York: Basic Books, 1971), p. 286.

5. Nancy Chodorow, *The Reproduction of Mothering* (Berkeley and Los Angeles: University of California Press, 1978), p. 181.

6. For example, in "The Economic Problem in Masochism," Freud limits his discussion of "feminine masochism" to evidence of this syndrome in *men*. See this essay in *General Psychological Theory* (New York: Collier Books, 1963), especially p. 192.

7. Walshok, *Blue-Collar Women,* p. 7.

8. Martin Binkin and Shirley J. Bach, *Women and the Military* (Washington, D.C.: Brookings Institution, 1977), p. 32.

9. On the integration of the legal profession, see Cynthia Fuchs Epstein, *Women in Law* (New York: Basic Books, 1981). On the transformation of clerical work to "women's work," see Samuel Cohn, *The Process of Occupational Sex-Typing* (Philadelphia: Temple University Press, 1985), and Meta Zimmeck, "Jobs for the Girls: The Expansion of Clerical Work for Women, 1850–1914," in *Unequal Opportunities,* ed. Angela V. John (New York: Basil Blackwell, 1986), pp. 153–78. On the integration of the medical profession, see Gena Corea, *The Hidden Malpractice: How American Medicine Treats Women as Patients and Professionals* (New York: Morrow, 1977). Each of these studies shows that women eagerly flocked to apply for these various "nontraditional" occupations once official barriers to their admission had been eliminated.

10. Cohn, *The Process,* p. 230.

11. Barbara Melosh, *"The Physician's Hand": Work Culture and Conflict in American Nursing* (Philadelphia: Temple University Press, 1982), p. 66.

12. Barbara Ehrenreich and Deirdre English, *Witches, Midwives*

and Nurses: A History of Women Healers (Oyster Bay, N.Y.: Glass Mountain Pamphlets, n.d.).

13. Ann Game and Rosemary Pringle, *Gender at Work* (Sydney: Allen and Unwin, 1983), pp. 94, 111.

14. Reskin and Hartmann, *Women's Work,* p. 128.

15. Deaux and Ullman, *Women of Steel,* p. 165.

16. Richard A. Gabriel, "Women in Combat?" *Army,* March 1980, p. 50.

METHODOLOGICAL APPENDIX

1. Some problems encountered by female researchers interviewing male respondents are discussed in Lorna McKee and Margaret O'Brien, "Interviewing Men: 'Taking Gender Seriously,' " in *The Public and the Private,* ed. Eva Gamarnikow et al. (London: Heinemann, 1983).

Bibliography

BOOKS AND ARTICLES

Aiken, Linda H., Roger Blendon, and David Rogers. "The Shortage of Hospital Nurses: A New Perspective." In *Nursing Issues and Nursing Strategies for the Eighties,* ed. Bonnie Bullough, Vern Bullough, and Mary Claire Soukup, pp. 22–38. New York: Springer, 1983.

Aldag, Jean C., and Cherryl Christensen. "Personality Correlates of Male Nurses." *Nursing Research* 16 (1967): 375–76.

American Nurses' Association. *Inventory of Registered Nurses, 1977–78.* Kansas City, Mo.: American Nurses' Association, 1981.

Anderson, Karen. *Wartime Women: Sex Roles, Family Relations and the Status of Women in World War II.* Westport, Conn.: Greenwood Press, 1981.

Arkin, William. "Military Socialization and Masculinity." *Journal of Social Issues* 34 (1978): 151–68.

Beck, B. G. "Women as Warriors: A Study in Contrasts." *Army,* February 1981, pp. 26 ff.

Beebe, Michael, Steve Barr, and Mary Hamilton. "Anatomy Is Destiny." In *Nursing Issues and Nursing Strategies for the Eighties,* ed. Bonnie Bullough, Vern Bullough, and Mary Claire Soukup, pp. 38–49. New York: Springer, 1983.

Beller, Andrea, and Kee-Ok Kim Han. "Occupational Sex Segregation: Prospects for the 1980s." In *Sex Segregation in the Workplace: Trends, Explanations, Remedies,* ed. Barbara Reskin, pp. 106–11. Washington, D.C.: National Academy Press, 1984.

Bernays, Edward L. "The Armed Services and the Nursing Profession." *American Journal of Nursing* 46:3 (March 1946): 166–69.

Bielby, William, and James N. Baron. "A Woman's Place Is with Other Women." In *Sex Segregation in the Workplace: Trends, Explanations, Remedies,* ed. Barbara Reskin, pp. 27–55. Washington, D.C.: National Academy Press, 1984.

Binkin, Martin, and Shirley J. Bach. *Women and the Military.* Washington, D.C.: Brookings Institution, 1977.

Briggs, W. P. "Men Nurses in the U.S. Navy." *American Journal of Nursing* 43 (1943): 39–42.

Brown, Daniel M. "Men Nurses and the U.S. Navy." *American Journal of Nursing* 42 (1942): 499–501.

Brown, Ronald G. S., and Robert W. H. Stones. *The Male Nurse.* London: G. Bell & Sons, 1973.

Bush, Patricia J. "The Male Nurse: A Challenge to Traditional Role Identities." *Nursing Forum* 15 (1976): 390–405.

Campbell, D'Ann. *Women at War with America: Private Lives in a Patriotic Era.* Cambridge, Mass.: Harvard University Press, 1984.

Carnegie, Mary Elizabeth. *The Path We Tread: Blacks in Nursing, 1854–1984.* Philadelphia: Lippincott, 1986.

Carrigan, Tim, Bob Connell, and John Lee. "Toward a New Sociology of Masculinity." *Theory and Society* 14 (September 1985): 551–603.

Chodorow, Nancy. "Being and Doing: A Cross-Cultural Examination of the Socialization of Males and Females." In *Women in Sexist Society,* ed. Vivian Gornick and Barbara Moran, pp. 259–91. New York: Basic Books, 1971.

———. "Gender, Relation, and Difference in Psycho-analytic Perspective." In *The Future of Difference,* ed. Hester Eisenstein and Alice Jardine, pp. 3–19. Boston: G. K. Hall, 1980.

———. *The Reproduction of Mothering: Psychoanalysis and the Sociol-*

ogy of Gender. Berkeley and Los Angeles: University of California Press, 1978.

Christman, Luther. "Men in Nursing: One Means to Efficiency in Care." *Pennsylvania Nurse,* September 1970, pp. 6ff.

Cleland, Virginia. "Sex Discrimination: Nursing's Most Pervasive Problem." *American Journal of Nursing* 71 (August 1971): 1542–47.

Cohn, Samuel. *The Process of Occupational Sex-Typing*. Philadelphia: Temple University Press, 1985.

Corea, Gena. *The Hidden Malpractice: How American Medicine Treats Women as Patients and Professionals*. New York: Morrow, 1977.

Deaux, Kay, and Joseph Ullman. *Women of Steel*. New York: Praeger, 1983.

de Beauvoir, Simone. *The Second Sex*. New York: Knopf, 1957.

Dolan, Josephine. *Nursing in Society,* 14th ed. Philadelphia: Saunders, 1978.

Douglas, Mary. "Institutionalized Public Memory." In *The Social Fabric: Dimensions and Issues,* ed. James F. Short, pp. 63–76. Beverly Hills, Calif.: Sage Publications, 1986.

Earley, Pete. "Women Ask If Army Is Going Off Limits." *Washington Post,* August 4, 1982, p. 17.

Ehrenreich, Barbara, and Deirdre English. *Witches, Midwives and Nurses: A History of Women Healers*. Oyster Bay, N.Y.: Glass Mountain Pamphlets, n.d.

Eisenhart, R. Wayne. "You Can't Hack It, Little Girl: A Discussion of the Covert Psychological Agenda of Modern Combat Training." *Journal of Social Issues* 31 (1975): 13–25.

Enloe, Cynthia. *Does Khaki Become You?: The Militarization of Women's Lives*. London: Pluto Press, 1983.

Epstein, Cynthia Fuchs. *Women in Law*. New York: Basic Books, 1981.

Fitzpatrick, M. Louise. "Nursing." *Signs* 2:4 (Summer 1977): 818–34.

Floge, Liliane, and Deborah M. Merrill. "Tokenism Reconsidered: Male Nurses and Female Physicians in a Hospital Setting." Paper presented at the 80th meeting of the American Sociological Association, Washington, D.C., August 28, 1985.

Foner, Jack D. *Blacks and the Military in American History.* New York: Praeger, 1974.

Fottler, Myron D. "Attitudes of Female Nurses Toward the Male Nurse: A Study of Occupational Segregation." *Journal of Health and Social Behavior* 17 (June 1976): 99–111.

Freud, Sigmund. "Analysis Terminable and Interminable" (1937). In *The Standard Edition of the Complete Psychological Works of Sigmund Freud,* ed. James Strachey, pp. 209–54. London: Hogarth Press, 1964.

———. "Dissection of the Psychical Personality" (1933). In *New Introductory Lectures on Psychoanalysis,* pp. 51–71. New York: Norton, 1965.

———. "The Economic Problem in Masochism." In *General Psychological Theory,* pp. 190–201. New York: Collier, 1963.

———. "Femininity" (1933). In *New Introductory Lectures on Psychoanalysis,* pp. 99–119. New York: Norton, 1965.

———. "The Passing of the Oedipus-Complex." In *Sexuality and the Psychology of Love,* pp. 176–82. New York: Collier, 1963.

———. "Some Psychological Consequences of the Anatomical Distinction Between the Sexes" (1925). In *Sexuality and the Psychology of Love,* pp. 183–93. New York: Collier, 1963.

Gabriel, Richard A. "Women in Combat?" *Army,* March 1980, pp. 45ff.

Gamarnikow, Eva. "Sexual Division of Labour: The Case of Nursing." In *Feminism and Materialism,* ed. Annette Kuhn and AnnMarie Wolpe, pp. 96–123. London: Routledge and Kegan Paul, 1978.

Game, Ann, and Rosemary Pringle. *Gender at Work.* Sydney: Allen and Unwin, 1983.

Gans, Janet E. "The Mobile Minority: Men's Success in a Woman's Profession." Ph.D. dissertation, University of Massachusetts, 1984.

————. "Sex Differences in Tokens' Career Attainment." Paper presented at the 1983 annual meeting of the Society for the Study of Social Problems, Detroit, Michigan, 1983.

Garfinkel, Harold. *Studies in Ethnomethodology.* Englewood Cliffs, N.J.: Prentice-Hall, 1967.

Garvin, Bonnie J. "Values of Male Nursing Students." *Nursing Research* 25:5 (September 1976): 352–57.

Greenberg, Emily, and Burton Levine. "Role Strain in Men Nurses." *Nursing Forum* 10 (1971): 416–30.

Groff, Ben. "The Trouble with Male Nursing." *American Journal of Nursing* 84:1 (January 1984): 62–63.

Hartmann, Heidi. "The Family as Locus of Gender, Class, and Political Struggle: The Example of Housework." *Signs* 6:3 (Spring 1981): 366–94.

————. "The Unhappy Marriage of Marxism and Feminism." *Capital and Class* 8 (1979): 1–33.

Hartmann, Susan M. *The Home Front and Beyond: American Women in the 1940's.* Boston: Twayne, 1982.

————. "Women in the Military Service." In *Clio Was a Woman,* ed. Mabel E. Deutrich and Virginia C. Purdy, pp. 195–205. Washington, D.C.: Howard University Press, 1980.

Hesselbart, S. "Women Doctors Win and Male Nurses Lose." *Sociology of Work and Occupations* 4 (1977): 49–62.

Hicks, Jack. "Women in the Army." *Armed Forces and Society* 4:4 (August 1978): 647–57.

Hine, Darlene Clark. "Mabel K. Staupers and the Integration of Black Nurses into the Armed Forces." In *Black Leaders of the Twentieth Century,* ed. John Hope Franklin and August Meier, pp. 241–57. Urbana: University of Illinois Press, 1982.

Holm, Jeanne. *Women in the Military: An Unfinished Revolution.* Novato, Calif.: Presidio Press, 1982.

Holtzclaw, Barbara J. "The Man in Nursing: Relationship Between Sex-Typed Perceptions and Locus of Control." Ph.D. dissertation, University of Oklahoma, School of Nursing, 1984.

Honey, Maureen. *Creating Rosie the Riveter: Class, Gender, and*

Propaganda During World War II. Amherst: University of Massachusetts Press, 1984.

Hughes, Linda. "The Public Image of the Nurse." *Advances in Nursing Science* 2:3 (April 1980): 55–72.

Hull, Richard T. "Dealing with Sexism in Nursing and Medicine." *Nursing Outlook,* February 1982, pp. 89–94.

Jamieson, Elizabeth, Mary Sewall, and Lucille S. Gjertson. *Trends in Nursing History*. Philadelphia: Saunders, 1959.

Johnston, Thomas. "The Sexist in Nursing: Who Is She?" *Nursing Forum* 18 (1979): 204–5.

Jones, Kathleen. "Dividing the Ranks: Women and the Draft." *Women & Politics* 4:4 (Winter 1985): 75–87.

Kalisch, Philip A., and Beatrice J. Kalisch. *The Advance of American Nursing*. Boston: Little, Brown, 1978.

———. *Politics of Nursing*. Philadelphia: Lippincott, 1982.

Kalisch, Philip A., and Margaret Scobey. "Female Nurses in American Wars: Helplessness Suspended for the Duration." *Armed Forces and Society* 9:2 (Winter 1983): 215–44.

Kanter, Rosabeth Moss. *Men and Women of the Corporation*. New York: Basic Books, 1977.

———. "Some Effects of Proportions on Group Life: Skewed Sex Ratios and Responses to Token Women." *American Journal of Sociology* 82 (March 1977): 965–90.

Keil, Sally Van Wagenen. *Those Wonderful Women in Their Flying Machines: The Unknown Heroines of World War II*. New York: Wade Publishers, 1979.

Kerce, Elyse W., and Marjorie H. Royle. *First-Term Enlisted Marine Corps Women: Their Backgrounds and Experiences*. San Diego, Calif.: Navy Personnel Research and Development Center, 1984.

Kessler, Doris H. (Maj.), and (Maj.) Richard A. Gabriel. "Women in Combat? Two Views." *Army,* March 1980, pp. 44ff.

Kessler, Suzanne, and Wendy McKenna. *Gender: An Ethnomethodological Approach*. New York: Wiley, 1978.

Kramer, Marlene, and Constance Baker. "The Exodus: Can We Prevent It?" *Journal of Nursing Administration* 1 (1971): 15–30.

Lipman-Bluman, Jean. *Gender Roles and Power*. Englewood Cliffs, N.J.: Prentice-Hall, 1984.

McCarragher, James A. "Attitudes of Nurses Toward the Male Nurse: A Question of Stigma." Master's thesis, Case Western Reserve University, 1984.

McCarty, P. "Survey Shows a Million RN's Are Employed." *American Nurse* 12 (1980): 1, 6, 10.

McKee, Lorna, and Margaret O'Brien. "Interviewing Men: 'Taking Gender Seriously.' " In *The Public and the Private,* ed. Eva Gamarnikow et al. London: Heinemann, 1983.

Mannino, Sandy F. "The Professional Man Nurse: Why He Chose Nursing and Other Characteristics of Men in Nursing." *Nursing Research* 12:3 (Summer 1963): 185–87.

Mansbridge, Jane J. *Why We Lost the ERA*. Chicago: University of Chicago Press, 1986.

Marshall, Kathryn. "Who Are the Women Who Join the Marines?" *Ms.* 9:8 (February 1981): 52ff.

Melosh, Barbara. *"The Physician's Hand"*: *Work Culture and Conflict in American Nursing*. Philadelphia: Temple University Press, 1982.

Milkman, Ruth. *Gender at Work: The Dynamics of Job Segregation by Sex During World War II*. Urbana and Chicago: University of Illinois Press, 1987.

Minnigerode, Fred A., Jeanie S. Kasyer-Jones, and Gerard Garcia. "Masculinity and Femininity in Nursing." *Nursing Research* 27:5 (September–October 1978): 299–302.

Morgan, D. H. J. *Social Theory and the Family*. London: Routledge and Kegan Paul, 1975.

Muff, Janet, ed. *Socialization, Sexism, and Stereotyping: Women's Issues in Nursing*. St. Louis: Mosby, 1982.

Nabors, Robert L. "Women in the Army: Do They Measure Up?" *Military Review* 62:10 (October 1982): 50–61.

O'Brien, Tim. *If I Die in the Combat Zone*. New York: Dell, 1979.

Osborne, Estelle Massey. "Status and Contribution of the Negro Nurse." *Journal of Negro Education* 18 (Summer 1949): 364–69.

Parsons, Talcott. "The Superego and the Theory of Social Systems" (1952). In *Social Structure and Personality*, pp. 17–33. New York: Free Press, 1970.

———and Robert Bales. *Family: Socialization and Interaction Process*. Glencoe, Ill.: Free Press, 1955.

Pinch, Franklin C. "Military Manpower and Social Change: Assessing the Institutional Fit." *Armed Forces and Society* 8:4 (Summer 1982): 575–600.

Polatnick, Margaret. "Why Men Don't Rear Children: A Power Analysis." *Berkeley Journal of Sociology* 18 (1974): 45–86.

Quester, George H. "The Problem." In *Female Soldiers—Combatants or Noncombatants?*, ed. Nancy L. Goldman, pp. 217–35. Westport, Conn.: Greenwood Press, 1982.

Rapoport, Daniel. "Women in Combat." *National Journal*, July 17, 1982, p. 1266.

Reskin, Barbara F., and Heidi Hartmann, eds. *Women's Work, Men's Work: Sex Segregation on the Job*. Washington, D.C.: National Academy Press, 1986.

Reskin, Barbara, and Patricia Roos. "Status Hierarchies and Sex Segregation." In *Ingredients for Women's Employment Policy*, ed. Christine Bose and Glenna Spitze, pp. 3–21. Albany: State University of New York Press, 1987.

Roberts, Mary M. *American Nursing: History and Interpretation*. New York: Macmillan, 1954.

Rogan, Helen. *Mixed Company: Women in the Modern Army*. New York: Putnam's, 1981.

Rubin, Lillian. *Intimate Strangers*. New York: Harper and Row, 1983.

Rupp, Leila J. *Mobilizing Women for War: German and American Propaganda, 1939–1945*. Princeton, N.J.: Princeton University Press, 1979.

Rustad, Michael. *Women in Khaki: The American Enlisted Woman*. New York: Praeger, 1982.

Sadler, Georgia Clark. "Women in the Sea Services: 1972–1982." *U.S. Naval Institute Proceedings 109/5/963* (1983): 140–55.

Savell, Joel M. "A Study of Male and Female Soldiers' Beliefs About the 'Appropriateness' of Various Jobs for Women in the Army." *Sex Roles 5* (1979): 41–50.

Schoenmaker, Adrian. "Nursing's Dilemma: Male Versus Female Admissions Choice." *Nursing Forum 15* (1976): 406–12.

Schoenmaker, Adrian, and David M. Radosevich. "Men Nursing Students: How They Perceive Their Situation." *Nursing Outlook 24* (May 1976): 299.

Schroedel, Jean Reith. *Alone in a Crowd: Women in the Trades Tell Their Stories*. Philadelphia: Temple University Press, 1985.

Segal, Bernard E. "Male Nurses: A Case Study in Status Contradiction and Prestige Loss." *Social Forces 41* (1962): 31–38.

Segal, David. "The Concept of Citizenship and Attitudes Toward Women in Combat." *Sex Roles 3* (1977): 469–80.

Segal, Mady Wechsler. "The Argument for Female Combatants." In *Female Soldiers—Combatants or Noncombatants?,* ed. Nancy L. Goldman, pp. 267–90. Westport, Conn.: Greenwood Press, 1982.

———. "Women's Roles in the U.S. Armed Forces: An Evaluation of Evidence and Arguments for Policy Decisions." In *Conscripts and Volunteers,* ed. Robert K. Fullinwider, pp. 200–13. Totowa, N.J.: Rowman and Allenheld, 1983.

Stiehm, Judith Hicks. *Bring Me Men and Women: Mandated Change at the U.S. Air Force Academy*. Berkeley and Los Angeles: University of California Press, 1981.

———. "The Protected, the Protector, the Defender." *Women's Studies International Forum 5*:3/4 (1982): 367–76.

Stoller, Robert J. *Presentations of Gender*. New Haven, Conn.: Yale University Press, 1985.

———. *Sex and Gender: On the Development of Masculinity and Femininity*. New York: Science House, 1968.

Treadwell, Mattie E. *The Women's Army Corps.* Washington, D.C.:
U.S. Army, Office of Military History, 1954.

Tumminia, Patricia A. "Teaching Problems and Strategies with
Male Nursing Students." *Nurse Educator* (September–October
1981): 9–11.

Tuten, Jeff M. "The Argument Against Female Combatants." In
Female Soldiers—Combatants or Noncombatants?, ed. Nancy L.
Goldman, pp. 237–65. Westport, Conn.: Greenwood Press,
1982.

U.S. Army Research Institute. *Women Content in Units Force Development Test (MAXWAC).* 1977.

U.S. Department of Defense. Manpower Installations and Logistics. *Military Women in the Department of Defense.* 1984.

U.S. Department of Defense. Office of the Assistant Secretary of
Defense (Manpower, Reserve Affairs, and Logistics). *Use of
Women in the Military,* rev. 2nd ed. September 1978.

———. *Profile of American Youth.* 1982.

U.S. Department of Defense. Office of the Deputy Assistant Secretary of Defense for Equal Opportunity and Safety Policy. *Black
Americans in Defense of Our Nation.* Washington, D.C.: Government Printing Office, 1985.

U.S. Department of Health and Human Services. Public Health
Service. *Minorities and Women in the Health Fields.* Washington, D.C.: Government Printing Office, 1984.

U.S. Department of the Army. Office of the Deputy Chief of Staff
for Personnel. *Evaluation of Women in the Army (EWITA).*
1978.

———. *Women in the Army Policy Review.* 1982.

U.S. House of Representatives. *Appendix to the Congressional Record.* "Why not use male nurses?," remarks of Hon. Walter H.
Judd (February 26, 1945): A838.

———. *Congressional Record.* Debate to establish the W.A.A.C.
(March 17, 1942): 2580–608.

———. *Congressional Record.* Nurses Selective Service Bill of 1945
(March 5, 1945): 1725–44.

———. Committee on Armed Services. Subcommittee No. 2.

Hearings. Subcommittee Hearings on H.R. 2559 (Thursday, July 7, 1955): 4289–305.

U.S. Marine Corps. Marine Corps Institute. *The United States Marine—Essential Subjects.* 1983.

U.S. Office of the President. Military Manpower Task Force. *A Report to the President on the Status of the All-Volunteer Force,* rev. ed. Washington, D.C.: Government Printing Office, 1982.

Vaz, Dolores. "High School Senior Boys' Attitudes Towards Nursing as a Career." *Nursing Research* 17:6 (November–December 1968): 533–38.

Walshok, Mary Lindenstein. *Blue Collar Women: Pioneers on the Male Frontier.* Garden City, N.Y.: Anchor Press, 1981.

Willenz, June A. *Women Veterans: America's Forgotten Heroines.* New York: Continuum, 1983.

Wilson, Ruth Danenhower. *Jim Crow Joins Up.* New York: Clark, 1944.

Wilson, Victoria. "An Analysis of Femininity in Nursing." *American Behavioral Scientist* 15:2 (November–December 1971): 213–20.

Woelfel, John C. "Women in the United States Army." *Sex Roles* 7 (1981): 785–800.

Women's Equity Action League. *WEAL Facts.* 1984.

Wright, Michael. "The Marine Corps Faces the Future." *New York Times Magazine,* June 20, 1982, pp. 16ff.

Zimmeck, Meta. "Jobs for the Girls: The Expansion of Clerical Work for Women, 1850–1914." In *Unequal Opportunities,* ed. Angela V. John, pp. 153–78. New York: Basil Blackwell, 1986.

PERIODICALS CITED

The American Journal of Nursing
Army Times
Baltimore Sun
Christian Science Monitor
Facts About Nursing (American Nurses' Association)
Jacksonville Journal (Florida)

Los Angeles Times
The Marine Corps Gazette
Navy Times
The New York Times
Oakland Tribune (California)
Regan Report on Nursing Law
San Francisco Chronicle
Time
Washington Post

Index

Abortion, 23
Acquired immune deficiency syndrome (AIDS), 122
Acute care, male nurses in, 95, 113–14, 120, 121
Administration, male nurses in, 9, 90, 113–14, 125, 129–30, 132
Affirmative action, 125–26, 142–43
Age: in military, 21, 35–36; of nurses, 35–36, 112
Aggressiveness, male nurses and, 126–27, 129–30
Aiken, Linda H., 164n.39
Air force: combat exclusionary policies in, 50, 53, 54, 84; in Grenada invasion, 158–59n.19; harassment in, 70; male gender identity threatened in, 64; in study sample, 16, 145
Air Force Academy, 64, 70
Aldag, Jean C., 163n.30
American Assembly for Men in Nursing (AAMN), 18, 104, 118, 146–47
American Journal of Nursing, 157nn.42, 44, 46, 47, 48, 49
American Nurses' Association (ANA): and black nurses, 37; cited, 161nn.2, 7, 163n.38,

164nn.39, 41; and male nurses, 40, 93–94, 102, 103; and military nurses, 34, 40, 93–94
American Psychiatric Association, 91, 93
Anesthetists, nurse, 129
Antiaircraft Artillery (AAA), 26–27
Army: attrition rates in, 58; cited, 159nn.31, 32; combat exclusionary policies in, 57–58; discrimination in, 47–48; entrance standards for, 46; femininity in, 161n.58; and homosexuality, 155n.21; integration in, 56–57, 60–61, 143; nurses in, 20, 23, 34–35, 38, 40, 92, 93; reasons for joining, 72; studies on women in, 49–50, 56, 57–58
Army Nursing Corps (ANC), 20, 23, 34–35, 38, 40, 92, 93
Army Research Institute, 49, 157–58nn.7, 8
Army Times, 159nn.23, 33
Attrition rates: military, 52, 58, 59; in nursing, 124–25, 164n.39
Australia, male nurses in, 142
Auto mechanics, 2
Auxiliaries, military, 21–34

New York Times, 155n.27,
159n.36
Nightingale, Florence, 2
Nontraditional occupations, 2–8,
139–40, 142, 165n.9; dress
in, 4, 62–63, 115; gender identity concerns in, 134–35 (*see
also* Femininity; Masculinity);
gender maintenance and, 9,
131–32; in military, 20, 24–
25, 26–27, 33, 58–59 (*see also*
Female marines); status in,
109, 132–33; World War II
nonmilitary, 25. *See also* Female marines; Male nurses
"Normalcy": of female marines,
71; of gender identity, 7
Numerical rarity, in occupations,
4, 98, 131
Nursing, 18; attrition rates in,
124–25, 164n.39; laws related
to, 35, 36, 92–94; in military,
20, 23, 34–43, 88–89, 92,
93–95, 122–23, 138,
156nn.34, 38; specialties in, 4,
40, 91, 93, 94, 95, 113–32
passim. *See also* Female nurses;
Male nurses; Schools, nursing

O'Brien, Margaret, 166n.1
Obstetrics, males nurses and, 4,
95, 117, 120
Occupational integration. *See* Integration
Occupational segregation, 2–6,
131, 133, 141–43; internal, 3,
10, 138–39 (*see also* Informal
practices); in military, 19–34
passim, 51, 52, 57–69 passim,
82–83, 94, 132, 138–39,
155n.20; nursing and, 19, 91,

94, 115, 117–19, 138–39,
140–41, 156n.40. *See also* Nontraditional occupations; Positions; Specialties; Traditional
occupations
Occupations: nontraditional, *see*
Nontraditional occupations; in
nursing, *see* Female nurses,
Male nurses; sex-segregated, *see*
Occupational segregation; traditional, 2, 25, 33–34, 51. *See
also* Military
Ohio Nursing Association, 98–99
Osborne, Estelle Massey, 156n.40

Parris Island, South Carolina, 16,
17, 63, 70–71, 145, 146
Parsons, Talcott, 11, 153–
54nn.20, 21
Patients, and male nurses, 40,
101, 105–7, 119–20
Patriotism, as reason for joining
marines, 28
Pay: in men's jobs, 132; military,
35, 39, 56, 139; in nursing,
35, 95–96, 102, 124–25, 129,
135, 141
Physical strength: male nurses
and, 101, 116–17, 119; military and, 52, 53–54, 62, 71
Physicians: female, 105, 139; males
being nurses instead of, 110–
12; nurses interacting with,
103–5, 118–19, 125, 130
Pilots, 2, 16, 53. *See also* Air force
Poise, female marine, 63, 66, 78,
160n.45
Polatnick, Margaret, 153n.16
Population by sex: in military, 2,
34, 45, 50, 51, 55–56; in nursing, 2, 34, 88, 89

Compositor: Huron Valley Graphics
Text: Galliard 10/13
Display: Galliard
Printer: Maple-Vail Book Mfg. Group
Binder: Maple-Vail Book Mfg. Group